100
ways to
enhance
self-concept
in the
classroom

related titles of interest

Clearly Outstanding: Making Each Day Count in Your Classroom
Gary D. Borich
ISBN: 0-205-13332-0

101 Ways to Develop Student Self-Esteem and Responsibility, The Teacher as Coach, Volume I
Jack Canfield and Frank Siccone
ISBN: 0-205-13368-1 Paper   0-205-13370-3 Cloth

101 Ways to Develop Student Self-Esteem and Responsibility, The Power to Succeed in School and Beyond, Volume II
Frank Siccone and Jack Canfield
ISBN: 0-205-14068-8 Paper   0-205-14067-X Cloth

Teaching Social Skills to Children: Innovative Approaches, Second Edition
Gwendolyn Cartledge and JoAnne Fellows Milburn (Editors)
ISBN: 0-205-14299-0 Paper   0-205-14300-8 Cloth

Self-Esteem Enhancement with Children and Adolescents
Alice W. Pope, Susan M. McHale, and W. Edward Craighead
ISBN: 0-205-14455-1 Paper   0-205-14456-X Cloth

Winners Without Losers: Structures and Strategies for Increasing Student Motivation to Learn
James P. Raffini
ISBN: 0-205-14008-4

Jack Canfield
President, Self-Esteem Seminars,
Culver City, CA

Harold Clive Wells
Professor and
Vice President for Academic Affairs, Emeritus
National University, San Diego, CA

ALLYN AND BACON
Boston   London   Toronto   Sydney   Tokyo   Singapore

second edition

100

ways to enhance self-concept in the classroom

a handbook for teachers, counselors, and group leaders

This book is dedicated to
teachers, counselors, and everyone
committed to helping children develop
a true sense of themselves
as lovable and capable human beings.

Copyright © 1994, 1976 by Allyn and Bacon
A Division of Simon & Schuster, Inc.
160 Gould Street
Needham Heights, Massachusetts 02194

Library of Congress Cataloging-in-Publication Data
Canfield, Jack
   100 ways to enhance self-concept in the classroom : a handbook for
teachers, counselors, and group leaders / Jack Canfield, Harold
Clive Wells. -- 2nd ed.
     p.   cm.
   Includes bibliographical references (p.).
   ISBN 0-205-15711-4. -- ISBN 0-205-15415-8 (pbk.)
   1. Motivation in education.   2. Self-actualization (Psychology)
3. Self-respect.   I. Wells, Harold Clive.   II. Title.
III. Title: One hundred ways to enhance self-concept in the
classroom.
LB1065.C26   1994
370.15'4--dc20
                                         93-23393
                                            CIP

We wish to acknowledge many publishers and individuals for their permission to reprint materials in this book; since there is insufficient space to accommodate them here, we have done so beginning on page xiv.

Printed in the United States of America
10 9 8 7   98 99 00 01

contents

foreword   Sidney B. Simon   **xi**

introduction: self-concept in teaching and learning   **1**

a note to teachers on how to use this book   **9**
Children Learn What They Live   Dorothy Law Nolte   **12**

a note to counselors and group leaders   **15**

one   **getting started: building an environment of positive support**   **17**
   Love and the Cabbie   Art Buchwald   **17**
1   **the journal**   **21**
2   **that's the story of my life!**   **24**
3   **autobiographical questionnaires**   **26**
4   **ten questions**   **28**
5   **collage of self**   **30**
6   **the name game**   **33**
7   **my values bank**   **34**
8   **autobiographical sharing**   **37**
9   **getting to know you**   **38**
10   **success recall**   **40**
11   **success sharing**   **43**
12   **the magic box**   **44**
13   **hotshots**   **45**
14   **values sharing**   **47**
   Values Survey—Instrumental Values   **49**
   Values Survey—Terminal Values   **50**
15   **pride line**   **53**
   What Is a Native American?   Wa-Shea-Kwu   **54**
16   **success a day**   **55**
17   **personal coat-of-arms**   **57**
18   **personal flag**   **59**
19   **ball of yarn**   **60**
20   **self-portrait**   **63**
21   **success symbols**   **65**

contents

_____

22 what's my bag?   66
    Feelings List   68
23 becoming aware of feelings   69
24 one-way feeling glasses   73
25 meaningful symbols   75
26 object sharing   77
27 those nasty put downs   78
28 you can quote me on this!   80
29 dear me letter   83
30 re-entry questions   85
31 accurate listening—for content and feelings   87
32 an academic strategy   91
33 verbal martial arts   93
    Words That Encourage Dr. William Halton   96
34 positive reinforcement: an instructional solution   97
35 quickies   99

two my strengths   101
    The Animal School Dr. George H. Reavis   102

36 IALAC   103
37 personal evaluation sheet   109
38 strength bombardment   111
39 learning from failure   113
    Abraham Lincoln Didn't Quit   115
40 student of the week   116
    The B.E.S.T. Pledge   116
41 "I can't" funeral   118
42 nicknames   120
43 what's in a name?   122
44 going to Boston   123
45 commercial for oneself   125
46 positive support techniques   127

three who am I?   129
    About School Anonymous   130

47 owl game   133
48 voting . . . & additional questions   134
49 the ideal model   137
50 act as if   140
    My Personal Strengths Sheets   142
51 adjective wardrobe   144
52 if I were . . .   146
53 if I could be . . .   147

54 what if . . .   148
55 I used to be . . . but now I'm . . .   149
56 twenty things I like to do   150
57 . . . the eye of the beholder   151
58 one of a kind   153
59 who's who   155
60 how do I want to be today?   156
61 public interview   159
62 the public statement   161
63 motorcycle fantasy   163

four accepting my body   165

64 oh nose, I love you!   167
65 some body games   169
66 student photographs   173
67 fingerprints   175
68 the affectionate laying on of hands   176
69 the trust walk   177
70 body tracing   179
71 seven for the road   180
72 I love myself   182
73 sensory awareness   185
74 weather report   187
75 why I like myself   188

five where am I going?   191
      The Ten Steps to Success   191

76 twenty-one questions   194
77 four drawings   197
78 the goalpost   199
78a guidelines for goalsetting   200
      I Have a Dream   Martin Luther King   202
79 I have a dream   203
80 I have a dream—visualization   204
81 I have a dream—making it happen   207
82 on course/off course—a guidance system   209
83 five years ahead: resume   212
84 the six o'clock news   213

six the language of self   215

85 reframing hurtful assumptions   216
86 words that describe me   218
87 I am not my description   221
88 the tyranny of "should"   222

contents

89   scientific language   **224**
90   volunteering   **226**
91   whack the vulture   **229**
92   I can't . . . I won't   **231**
93   please . . . no!; yes . . . no!   **233**
94   incredible affirmations   **234**
95   identity, connectedness, and power   **237**

seven   relationships with others   **241**

96   the family   **242**
97   making friends   **245**
98   love notes   **249**
99   class applause   **251**
100   the car wash   **252**
101   hand massaging   **253**
    The Key to Health, Wealth, and Longevity   Dr. Joyce Brothers **254**
102   say hello to EVLN   **255**
103   making your wants known   **259**

eight   in closing—   **261**

nine   annotated bibliography of the best available resources   **263**

foreword

This book is an absolute delight! It is, indeed, a gold mine for teachers but it deserves a better metaphor than that cliché. It is more like cherry pie with so many damn cherries you can't get your fork through to the crust or pistachio ice cream so nutty no cone can handle it.

Jack Canfield and Harold Wells have compiled some of the sweetest, most gentle, most instantly useful and gripping exercises, strategies, and techniques ever put between the covers of a book. Their long, their lifelong, experiences with the humanistic education movement and their dedication to the notion that *positiveness* makes people grow illuminates every page of this book. The book glows and shines.

I warn you about one vital thing. Don't you dare read this book in summer, or on vacation, or on Friday night of a long weekend. The results could be dangerous. Why? And well you might ask. Why? Because you won't be able to stand the ordeal of not having your students in front of you to try out everything, immediately, in this exciting, practical, and deeply inspiring book. Be well warned.

The average teacher will find the concise clarity of the descriptions of each strategy almost magical. These writers don't just talk. It is apparent that they've *done* these exercises and they believe in them. (I would like to make an important cautionary note here. I, personally, urge every teacher using the strategies and techniques that Canfield and Wells have put before you here with such gemlike perfection to try the techniques, *first*, on your own life and experiences. That is, do the strategy and see what it brings out about your own life before you try these on other people's children. That seems like a decent enough ethical demand to make of you.)

This book is a lot more than just exercises, although there are, indeed, 100, count them, 100 beautiful examples of how to build a validating, searching positive and success-oriented community in any classroom.

The book includes an excellent bibliography and resource guide, which demonstrates how well grounded Canfield and Wells are in the humanistic education field. The back of the book becomes almost a road map for an individual teacher's growth. There are places to write to for curriculum guides, and there is a very useful guide to growth centers and other places where teachers can learn, stretch, and, hopefully, more fully come to reach their own very beautiful potential.

The profession needs, desperately, more practical, demonstratedly successful classroom materials like the ones so artfully brought together by Jack Canfield and Harold Wells. I am proud to be able to recommend this one so warmly.

It belongs in the Christmas stocking of every teacher in America. But, oops, remember my warning. If they get this book at Christmas, they won't have their students in front of them to try out the strategies. A warning could be put on the cover of every copy: "**CAUTION: Do Not Read Unless Teaching This Day.**" It would be just too frustrating to read the ideas and not have those live minds in front of you. Maybe a better idea would be if every superintendent of schools put one in every teachers' mailbox on the first day of school in September. If not then, then in January. The book is that great. Use it tenderly. And watch your self-concept grow. Joy.

Sidney B. Simon
Professor Emeritus of Humanistic Education, University of Massachusetts
School of Education, Amherst, Massachusetts

Two ancient and honorable kinds of love [are required of teachers]. The first is love of learning itself. . . . And the second kind of love on which this community depends is love of learners, of those we see every day, who stumble and crumble, who wax hot and cold, who sometimes want truth and sometimes evade it at all costs, but who are in our care, and who—for their sake, ours, and the world's—deserve all the love that the community of teaching and learning has to offer.

Parker J. Palmer, *Community, Conflict, and Ways of Knowing*

That's what's needed don't you see, that . . . nothing else matters half so much . . . to reassure one another, to answer each other. Perhaps only you can listen to me and not laugh. Everyone has inside himself . . . what shall I call it—a piece of good news. Everyone is a very great and important character. Yes, that's what we have to tell them. Every man must be persuaded, even if he's in rags, that he is immensely, immensely important. Everyone must respect him and make him respect himself, too. They must listen to him attentively—don't stand on top of him, don't stand in his light, but look at him with gentleness, deference; give him great, great hopes; he needs them, especially if he's young—spoil him. Yes, make him grow proud.

Ugo Betti, *Burnt Flower Bed* (an Italian play)

Children who have strong perceptions of closeness and trust with significant adults are highly resistant to peer influence and are more heavily influenced by those adults who validate them for who they are.

H. Stephen Glenn and Jane Nelson,
Raising Self-Reliant Children in a Self-Indulgent World

introduction: self-concept in teaching and learning

l am happy. l am sick. l am good. l am beautiful.
 I'm a loser. I'm a winner. I am dumb. I am fine.
I'm okay. I am bad. I am clumsy. I am a gossip.
 I'm neurotic. I am a bore. I'm a mess. I'm cool.
l am successful. I'm a failure. I'm lovable. I'm sexy.
 I am sad. I'm smart. I am a good teacher.
I am a good person. I'm a slow learner. I'm not okay.

Which of these sentences describe you? Go back and draw a circle around each sentence that expresses how you feel most of the time.

How many of your circled sentences please you? There are twenty-six sentences: thirteen that are essentially "positive" and thirteen "negative." When you look at your responses in this light, what kind of picture do you get of yourself? That picture is a little glimpse of a tiny part of your *self-concept!*

Your self-concept is composed of all the beliefs and attitudes you have about yourself. They actually determine *who you are!* They also determine *what* you think you are, what you *do,* and what you can *become!*

It's amazing to think that these internal beliefs and attitudes you hold about yourself are that powerful; but they are. In fact, in a very functional sense, they are your *Self.*

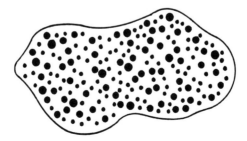

1

Imagine the "glob" on page 1 as a representation of your Self. You are an entity that hangs together in an organized, consistent, reasonably firm and permanent state, yet you also have the quality of fluidity—something like a strong jellyfish! The dots in the glob represent the thousands of beliefs you hold about yourself. They fit together in a meaningful pattern or "system," each complementing the others so that they form an integrated whole.

Notice that some of the dots are more "internal" than others. The more central a belief is to your Self, the more value—either negative or positive—you attach to it. For example, most teachers feel that to be smart is more important than to be a good swimmer. (Not everyone feels that way.) Most teachers' beliefs and attitudes about their own intelligence, then, are more central in their Self systems than their beliefs and attitudes about their swimming ability.

HOW IS THE SELF FORMED?

It is evident that the Self is learned. It is not inherited. From our earliest moments of life we begin to accumulate data about ourselves and our world. New impressions flood in upon us. We soon learn what eases pain and what makes us comfortable, what satisfies our hunger, what it takes to get attention, and so on. As our experiences multiply, our developing Self becomes a perceptual screen through which subsequent impressions must pass. For example, if an infant has been fed at the breast for weeks, he will not be satisfied with a spoon. His perceptual screen will reject the spoon as the wrong shape, and too hard and cold, and he will scream for the object he _knows_ is right!

In the same manner we gradually formulate impressions and attitudes about ourselves. A crawling baby reaches out to grasp a figurine on a low coffee table. The mother says, "No, no, no! Mustn't touch. Bad boy!" Repeated exposure to such responses teach the child—"I do things wrong. Things are more important than I am. I'm bad!" This, of course, is not at all what the parent wanted to teach, but nevertheless is precisely the message that many infants receive in such situations.

This example illustrates how vitally important early childhood experiences are in forming the kind of persons we become. We are especially vulnerable to the responses we get from our parents (particularly mother) because of the amount of time spent with them and our total dependence on them.

THE SELF IS CONSISTENT

Let's return to our illustration of the "glob." Any new experience you have is interpreted in light of all the beliefs and attitudes you've accumulated within your Self. If a new experience is consistent with what you believe, it is enveloped and your Self becomes a little larger. On the other hand, if the new experience is not consistent with your Self, it is ignored or rejected. Your "glob" simply withdraws a little where the new experience hits and moves right on past it, filling itself in as though nothing has occurred. This is a wonderful protective quality, actually. It keeps us together! There are some problems with it, however. It makes change in self-concept extremely difficult because to *significantly change anything* requires modification of the whole system in order to retain a consistency of Self. Here is an illustration of this concept:

Bennie is a good kid. He's a typical boy, so he sometimes gets into little scrapes, but never anything too bad. However, on this occasion Bennie is playing with some other boys and they decide to steal some cigarettes and hide somewhere and smoke them. Bennie is scared, but excited, too. Bennie's little brother hears about what has happened and tells their father, who raises the roof with poor Bennie. What does Bennie say? What does he really believe about the incident? "I didn't want to steal but—well, the gang kind of—you know. Besides I didn't steal the cigarettes. Charley did! I only smoked one and I hated it. It was a good lesson. I'll never smoke those awful things again."

Sounds like a lot of kids you know, doesn't it? Now why did Bennie respond like this? It's simple, really. Bennie, *just as every other human being alive, must protect his self-esteem—his feelings about himself.* He did that in this instance by rationalizing about being kind of "forced" into the situation and by figuring what a great lesson it was. He may, in time, actually come to believe he did it as an experiment; a lesson to himself on how bad cigarettes taste so he'll never again be tempted by the habit. See how smart that makes him, and how good he can feel about himself? So, two things have happened. First, Bennie's image of himself as a "good kid" is retained. He has taken an objectively "bad" incident and filtered it through his Self system in such a way as to maintain this consistency of his concept of himself. Second—and this is closely related—he has maintained or increased his self-esteem. *This is the prime motivation for all behavior.* It is perhaps our most important ability as human beings. We must, in spite of everything, be able to accept our own behavior. The strangest, most bizarre, and often most hideous behavior can be accounted for by this motivation to maintain and enhance one's Self *in one's own eyes.*

It is difficult for others to see how some behavior can possibly be Self-maintaining—but it is. We would have to be inside the skin of the other person to fully comprehend his actions, which of course is not possible, but we can keep this idea in mind and try to probe for data that will help us understand his rationale, no matter how distorted it may seem in *our* eyes.

WHAT YOU CAN DO ABOUT STUDENTS' SELF-CONCEPTS

Theory is helpful, but the heart of the matter is what we can **do** about students' self-concepts. We can extract several principles from what has been said above:

1. **It is possible to change self-concepts, possible for teachers to effect the changes—either way, both positive and negative.**
   Many of us teach because we had a teacher or two who really had a significant impact on us. The impact was related to our self-concept. The teacher somehow communicated a sense of caring and a sense of our own personal worth. On the other hand, many of us have also experienced a teacher who humiliated us or our classmates through sarcasm and ridicule. These teachers make learning a negative experience. Teachers can and do effect pupils' self-concepts every day. You have a choice over what kind of effect you will have.

2. **It isn't easy. Change takes place slowly, over a long period of time.**
   This is not written to discourage you, obviously, but simply to caution you not to expect sudden and dramatic changes in the way a child feels about himself. Self-concept builds the same way muscles do, slowly and often, at first, imperceptibly.

3. **Efforts that aim at more central beliefs have greater impact on students even though those beliefs are harder to change.**
   Our society puts very heavy emphasis on academic ability. If you can help the child see himself as capable of learning you are dealing with a central belief. If you help a mischievous boy see himself as kind and helpful, or a doubting girl see herself as intelligent and attractive, you've made a significant difference in the life of the child.

4. **Peripheral experiences are helpful.**
   Many successes are required to help a person feel better about himself in a basic sense. The development of talents is important, for example. Almost anything you do, from calling a student by his name to complimenting him on his new shoes helps to create a sense of self-worth.

5. **Relating successes or strengths to one another is important.**
   You can strengthen the impact of any enhancing experience by relating it to others the student has had. For example, when a child produces a good piece of art work, you can say, "I really like your picture, Tracy. You learned to use charcoal very quickly, I noticed!" This relates her artistic talent to what may be a more central belief about herself—her ability to learn.

CREATING AN OPEN, CARING ENVIRONMENT

Perhaps the most important thing a teacher can do to help students emotionally and intellectually is to create an environment of mutual support and caring. The crucial thing is the safety and encouragement students sense in the classroom. They must trust other group members and the teacher to the extent that they can truly express their feelings openly without ridicule or derision. Further, they must recognize that they are valued and will receive affection and support. This can't be stated strongly enough. Without the critical environmental dimensions of trust, caring, and openness, the teacher's efforts to enhance pupils' sense of self-esteem will be seriously limited.

Students have a vested interest in the emotional environment of the classroom as well. Teachers and students should sit down together and freely discuss cooperation and competition, trust and fear, openness and deceit, and so on. These and many other topics discussed in classroom meetings help create the kind of climate that fosters total pupil growth.

Abraham Maslow studied fully functioning or self-actualizing people. He described such emotionally healthy people by saying:

> Our teacher-subjects behaved in a very unneurotic way simply by interpreting the whole situation differently, i.e., as a pleasant collaboration rather than as a clash of wills, of authority, of dignity, etc. The replacement of artificial dignity—which is easily and inevitably threatened—with the natural simplicity which is not easily threatened; the giving up of the attempt to be omniscient and omnipotent; the absence of student-threatening authoritarianism, the refusal to regard the students as competing with each other or with the teacher; the refusal to assume the "professor" stereotype and the insistence on remaining as realistically human as, say a plumber or a carpenter; all of these created a classroom atmosphere in which suspicion, wariness, defensiveness, hostility, and anxiety disappeared.[1]

THE RELATIONSHIP OF SELF-CONCEPT TO LEARNING

One of the questions often asked by teachers regards the relationship of self-concept to the learning of subject matter. The research literature is filled with reports indicating that cognitive learning increases when self-concept increases. The data suggesting this conclusion is quite extensive and overwhelming.[2]

---

[1] Abraham H. Maslow, "Self-Actualizing People: A Study of Psychological Health," in Clark E. Moustakas, *The Self: Explorations in Personal Growth* (New York: Harper & Row, 1956), pp. 190–191.

[2] See Garry Walz and Jeanne Bleuer, *Students' Self-Esteem: A Vital Element of School Success* (Ann Arbor, MI: Counseling and Personnel Services, 1992).

By the time a child reaches school age his self-concept is quite well formed and his reactions to learning, to school failure and success, and to the physical, social, and emotional climate of the classroom will be determined by the beliefs and attitudes he has about himself. There is considerable evidence to support this view. Perhaps the most dramatic is that of Wattenberg and Clifford,[3] who studied kindergarten youngsters in an attempt to see if self-concept was predictive of reading success two and a half years later. It was. In fact, it was a better predictor than IQ! Children with low (poor) self-concepts did not learn to read or did not read as well as children with high (good) self-concepts.

Other studies affirm the position that self-concept is related to achievement in school; they also indicate that the relationship is particularly strong in boys, that it begins to make itself evident as early as the first grade, and that learning difficulties experienced in early school years persist.

THE POKER CHIP THEORY

We have developed a theory to explain this phenomenon which we call the "poker chip theory of learning." We see all learning as the result of a risk-taking situation somewhat akin to a poker game (or any other gambling situation, for that matter). In any potential learning situation, the student is asked to take a risk: to write a paper that will be evaluated, to make a recitation that may be laughed at, to do board work that may be wrong, to create an object of art that might be judged, etc. In each situation he is risking error, judgment, disapproval, censure, rejection, and, in extreme cases, even punishment. At a deeper level the student is risking his or her self-concept.

Imagine that each student's self-concept is a stack of poker chips. Some students start the learning game, as it were, with a lot of poker chips; others with very few. The students with the higher number of chips have a great advantage. To continue the poker analogy, the student with one hundred chips can sustain twenty losses of five chips each. The student with only fifteen chips can only sustain three losses of five chips each. The latter student will be much more cautious and reticent about stepping into the arena. This kind of student manifests a variety of behaviors indicating his reluctance to risk learning. They range from "This is stupid, I don't want to do it" (translation: "I am stupid; I'm afraid I can't do it") and withdrawn silence on one extreme to mischievous acting out on the other.

The student who has had a good deal of success in the past will be likely to risk success again; if he should fail, his self-concept can "afford" it. A student with a history predominated by failures will be reluctant to risk failure again. His depleted

---

[3] W. W. Wattenberg and C. Clifford, *Relationship of Self Concept to Beginning Achievement in Reading*, U.S. Office of Education, Cooperative Research Project No. 377 (Detroit: Wayne State University, 1962).

self-concept cannot afford it. Similar to someone living on a limited income, he will shop cautiously and look for bargains. One obvious recommendation in this situation is to make each learning step small enough so that the student is asked to only risk one chip at a time, instead of five. But even more obvious, in our eyes, is the need to build up the student's supply of poker chips so that he can begin to have a surplus of chips to risk.

If a student starts out, metaphorically speaking, with twenty chips and gains fifteen more through the exercises contained in this book, then, even if he loses ten in a reading class, he is still five ahead of the game. But if he loses ten from a starting position of twenty, he is now down to ten and in a very precarious psychological position. Viewed in this way, self-concept building can be seen as making sure that every student has enough chips to stay in the game.

In this book we offer you over 100 ways to build up each student's collection of chips![4]

A FINAL WORD ABOUT SELF-CONCEPT AND LEARNING

Students, like all of us, have a concept of themselves—as learners generally, and also as learners of specific subjects. It's probably every teacher's experience that some students see themselves as excellent in one subject but as struggling in another. This is one of the reasons schools and individual teachers, as well as parents, must provide a wide range of learning activities to find those areas in which each particular pupil can succeed.

It is also true that one's general self-esteem affects effort, which, in turn, affects success. We all must remember that *self-esteem is a by-product of accomplishment.* Success breeds success. So does diligence—plain hard work.

Students must forever be held to high standards—academically and behaviorally—and then given all of the encouragement and assistance possible to meet those standards. That assures high self-esteem. If the student is praised and rewarded for *effort* as well as achievement, the effort will lead to success.

When the 1992 U.S. Olympic basketball team—The Dream Team—was preparing for the Olympic games, the universal impression of the best of America's collegians who scrimmaged with them was the astonishing amount of time Magic Johnson, Larry Bird, and the others spent in *practice.* These players, among the greatest ever to play their sport, practiced hour after hour individually before and after *team* practices. In other words, they still realized the need to hone their skills even after reaching the pinnacle of success. And, of course, it was that kind of diligent practice that got them there in the first place.

---

[4] For a list of other materials currently available and workshops offered in the areas of affective education and self-esteem development, write to Self-Esteem Seminars, 6035 Bristol Parkway, Suite G, Culver City, CA 90230, or call (310) 337–9222 for faster service.

Students need to know that some sacrifices are required for success. In turn, they must be shown that time spent studying and practicing is not all drudgery. There is satisfaction and joy and pride in working to improve. The *process* of learning can be as uplifting as the result.

a note to teachers on how to use this book

WHEN TO USE THE EXERCISES

The question we are most asked by teachers who attend our workshops and classes is, "You know, I really think all of this is great, but with everything else I have to teach, where am I going to find time for this?" The practical experience of teachers who have used these materials indicates three general answers:

1. Many school systems, recognizing the awesome social problems of this era and the need for the holistic development of their students, have inaugurated new courses, sometimes required and sometimes elective, with titles like Human Development, Education of the Self, Human Relations, Project Self, The Search for Self, Basic Communication, The Human Potential Program, etc. In addition, health classes, drug and dropout prevention programs, and at-risk programs are providing desperately needed self-esteem building opportunities of the type found in this book. These classes explore various activities designed to help students understand and accept themselves better.

2. Where this is not possible because of rigid scheduling procedures, lack of budget, or lack of philosophical support on the part of the administration, another approach has worked well. This is to provide ten to twenty minutes every day or every other day to one or more of the exercises in the book. We usually suggest a heavier concentration during the first few weeks of school so that you can get things started off well, similar to the poker chip concept just mentioned. This regular ongoing activity can have a powerful effect on the classroom climate throughout the year. It can also provide the students with a cumulative, sequential, developmental curriculum in the affective domain—something sorely missing in our schools. It can also provide you with a greater feeling of excitement and energy as you experience what happens with your students. Our experience is that subject matter learning

has never suffered because of time spent on self-concept building. Quite to the contrary, it seems to be enhanced with the new self-confidence of the students.

3. A third approach is to use the activities whenever you have some free time—a rainy day, a canceled field trip, a class when your scheduled movie doesn't arrive, a period when your lesson plan only takes half the expected time, a day when the students just don't seem to be with it, etc. Another good experience we've had with the materials is when we've had to substitute for a sick teacher; rather than just having an extra study hall, we have used many of the exercises with a great deal of success and enjoyment.

You must understand that though this book is frequently written with a happy hand, and the activities in it are often lots of fun, they are by no means frivolous. It is intended that they be frequently repeated so participants can internalize the learning. Where one exercise is suggested to follow another, the reinforcing effects will be greatest if you attempt to follow the sequence. Raising a person's self-esteem requires that kind of diligence, persistence, and discipline.

HOW TO SEQUENCE THE ACTIVITIES

We have divided the activities into seven sections:

Getting Started

My Strengths

Who Am I?

Accepting My Body

Where Am I Going?

The Language of Self

Relationships with Others

The divisions seem to us to flow naturally one from the other. It is important to develop an environment of trust and support so that students will feel safe exploring themselves and interacting with each other (Part I). In order to begin to take risks and grow, they need to know where they are now and what their strengths are. They need to accept their present reality, including their bodies (Parts II, III, and IV). Then they need to have some sense of where they want to go, what they want to accomplish, and who they want to become (Part V). Part VI is devoted to understanding some of the ways children stop themselves from going where they want to go with their language. The last part is devoted to how students relate all of their emerging selves to others.

The activities within each section also have a natural sequence, which will become apparent as you use them. However, we are not advocating that you use the exercises in the order they appear. Some are more appropriate for one age level than another, some may seem redundant, some too complex for the time you have available, and so on. Read through several of the exercises in each section. Get a feel for what is available here. Then think about your class for a minute. What is primary right now? How do you feel about the emotional and self-concept climate of your classroom? What activities seem like they would be fun to do? Which ones do you think your students would respond to? Put all this data together and make a choice. Try it out and see what happens. What next step seems to be indicated by the responses of the students? Try that out, and so on. After a while the process of choosing activities will become a natural one. You'll find that you will begin to understand the assumptions upon which the activities are based and then you'll be inventing exercises and activities of your own.

THE TEACHER'S ATTITUDE

Throughout the book we refer to "accepting the students' responses without judgment" or maintaining a "nonjudgmental attitude." By this we mean that when a student shares an experience, a reaction, a feeling, a thought, or whatever, we must accept it as a true expression of his reality, his existence, or his awareness at that point in time. We may not always agree with what someone else does or says; that is because we perceive reality differently, or perhaps we are more evolved in our awareness, our level of consciousness. Owing to our unique set of past experiences we may have come to hold different values than our students. And that's O.K. That's who we are. The same is true of our students. That's who they are—unique individuals with differing views of themselves and their world. While we may be engaged in an endeavor to broaden their perceptions, heighten their awareness, and expand their consciousness, we must always respect their present state of being—which may be very different from ours.

If we are truly open to our students and accept them for who they are, then they too will begin to accept themselves as worthwhile beings—worthy of attention and love. There seems to be a natural and innate self-healing and self-actualizing process that occurs when one truly accepts oneself and the world as it is. Whole systems of psychology and many Eastern religious faiths are based on this single premise. We have observed the positive effects of such an approach in hundreds of classrooms with thousands of students.

We do not need to preach about "better ways of being" or moralize about how one *should* be. When we lecture students about themselves they tune us out, their defenses become stronger, and contact is blocked. We can ask them to examine the consequences of their behavior and to explore alternatives, but we have found that *it works better* to do this in the *nonjudgmental* spirit of broadening the student's options of choice rather than making him better because now he is somehow bad.

> A second-grade teacher in Iowa described her "encouragement approach" to teaching. While teaching her class cursive writing, she noticed one boy whose writing was totally indecipherable. She said that in the past she would have berated the boy for being lazy and incompetent. However, since choosing a self-esteem approach, she now says, "Johnny, this writing looks like it's getting a little better. I bet in a week we'll be able to make out at least one letter." A week later she was able to decipher several letters. She said, "I bet in a few weeks we'll be able to make out a whole word." Sure enough, it happened! The power of a positive expectation was working miracles with the boy. The teacher believed in him and he lived up to the expectation.

CHILDREN LEARN WHAT THEY LIVE
Dorothy Law Nolte

If a child lives with criticism,
    he learns to condemn.
If a child lives with hostility,
    he learns to fight.
If a child lives with fear,
    he learns to be apprehensive.
If a child lives with pity,
    he learns to feel sorry for himself.
If a child lives with ridicule,
    he learns to be shy.
If a child lives with jealousy,
    he learns what envy is.
If a child lives with shame,
    he learns to feel guilty.
If a child lives with encouragement,
    he learns to be confident.
If a child lives with tolerance,
    he learns to be patient.
If a child lives with praise,
    he learns to be appreciative.
If a child lives with acceptance,
    he learns to love.

If a child lives with approval,
  he learns to like himself.
If a child lives with recognition,
  he learns that it is good to have a goal.
If a child lives with sharing,
  he learns about generosity.
If a child lives with honesty and fairness,
  he learns what truth and justice are.
If a child lives with security,
  he learns to have faith in himself and in those about him.
If a child lives with friendliness,
  he learns that the world is a nice place in which to live.
If you live with serenity,
  your child will live with peace of mind.

With what is your child living?

a note to counselors and group leaders

Originally this book was subtitled *A Handbook for Teachers and Parents.* Our experience has been that parents have not had access to the book because it is not distributed through bookstores where parents normally select books.

School counselors and psychologists have often spoken to us about their successful use of the first edition, so we've changed the subtitle to reflect their interest. Group leaders of all sorts and flavors can use and have used this book in their work.

Teachers, of course, are group leaders. So are church school teachers, seminar and workshop leaders, and many people in business and industry who have found themselves training employees. Our experience is that all these folks can profitably use exercises in this book whether or not their specific interest is in the self-enhancement of their clients.

There are activities here that facilitate communication and sharing, that impel groups toward productive solutions, that serve to lessen tension and build consensus, and that help participants clarify their values—all very desirable goals for group leaders.

Counselors, psychologists, and group leaders need only to substitute the word *clients* or *participants* for *students*, and they can immediately apply most of the exercises. Appropriate selection and modification is easily within the capability of anyone who is qualified to be a counselor or lead a group.

A hundred years from now it will not matter what my bank account was, the sort of house I lived in, or the kind of car I drove. But, the world may be different because I was important in the life of a child.

Author Unknown

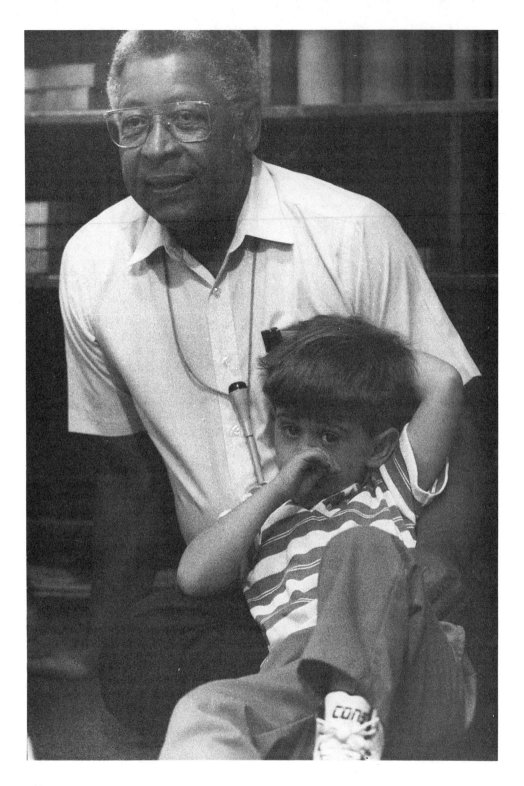

one

building an environment of positive support

As we said in the introduction, the exercises in this book will help you build a self-enhancing classroom climate. In part these start-up activities are designed for that purpose. They are simple, nonthreatening, and fun. They also begin the process of introspection, of getting into oneself to an extent not commonly experienced. They help the student become *aware* of himself in different dimensions. They indicate to him things in his life that make him proud. He sees that he surely has had some successes. He becomes aware of some of his deeper feelings and values.[1]

Besides beginning the task of creating a climate of positive support for class members and creating self-awareness, these activities contribute to the experience of one's identity. The student begins to see herself as a distinct and unique individual.

This is an especially critical time in our history for this kind of education; the alienation of youth, the loss of identity (or, as Eric Erikson calls it, "the identity crisis") of so many young people has resulted in severe social problems as well as individual loss of potential.

The activities suggested here contribute to growth rather than alienation when used by sensitive and empathic teachers. Use the ones that seem most appropriate to you for your group. They can only lead to better lives for youngsters. They begin the process that leads to a feeling of "I'm O.K.!"

LOVE AND THE CABBIE
Art Buchwald

I was in New York the other day and rode with a friend in a taxi. When we got out my friend said to the driver, "Thank you for the ride. You did a superb job of driving."

The taxi driver was stunned for a second. Then he said:

"Are you a wise guy or something?"

---

[1] For years, all formal writing used only masculine pronouns to refer to all students. In our view, this cultural norm has a subtle negative effect on the consciousness of female readers. In an attempt to deal with this problem in this book, we've alternated the use of masculine and feminine pronouns somewhat at random: sometimes from activity to activity and occasionally from paragraph to paragraph.

"No, my dear man, and I'm not putting you on. I admire the way you keep cool in heavy traffic."

"Yeh," the driver said and drove off.

"What was that all about?" I asked.

"I am trying to bring love back to New York," he said. "I believe it's the only thing that can save the city."

"How can one man save New York?"

"It's not one man. I believe I have made the taxi driver's day. Suppose he has 20 fares. He's going to be nice to those twenty fares because someone was nice to him. Those fares in turn will be kinder to their employees or shop-keepers or waiters or even their own families. Eventually the goodwill could spread to at least 1,000 people. Now that isn't bad, is it?"

"But you're depending on that taxi driver to pass your goodwill to others."

"I'm not depending on it," my friend said. "I'm aware that the system isn't foolproof so I might deal with 10 different people today. If, out of 10, I can make three happy, then eventually I can indirectly influence the attitudes of 3,000 more."

"It sounds good on paper," I admitted, "but I'm not sure it works in practice."

"Nothing is lost if it doesn't. I didn't take any of my time to tell that man he was doing a good job. He neither received a larger tip nor a smaller tip. If it fell on deaf ears, so what? Tomorrow there will be another taxi driver whom I can try to make happy."

"You're some kind of a nut," I said.

"That shows you how cynical you have become. I have made a study of this. The thing that seems to be lacking, besides money of course, for our postal employees, is that no one tells people who work for the post office what a good job they're doing."

"But they're not doing a good job."

"They're not doing a good job because they feel no one cares if they do or not. Why shouldn't someone say a kind word to them?"

We were walking past a structure in the process of being built and passed five workmen eating their lunch. My friend stopped. "That's a magnificent job you men have done. It must be difficult and dangerous work."

The five men eyed my friend suspiciously.

"When will it be finished?"

"June," a man grunted.

"Ah. That really is impressive. You must all be very proud."

We walked away. I said to him, "I haven't seen anyone like you since 'The Man from La Mancha.' "

"When those men digest my words, they will feel better for it. Somehow the city will benefit from their happiness."

"But you can't do this all alone!" I protested. "You're just one man."

"The most important thing is not to get discouraged. Making people in the city become kind again is not an easy job, but if I can enlist other people in my campaign. . ."

"You just winked at a very plain looking woman," I said.

"Yes, I know," he replied. "And if she's a schoolteacher, her class will be in for a fantastic day."

20

1 the journal

One way to most profitably use the exercises presented in this book is to have the students keep a journal of their reactions (feelings, thoughts, behaviors, "I learned . . ." statements, etc.) to each activity. Keeping a journal has several advantages. It allows the student to keep an ongoing account of how he is growing, of what is happening to him, of how he uniquely responds to a given situation. It provides a cumulative statement of who she is, how she sees herself, and how others see her.

The more a person learns about herself, the more she will expand her concept of herself. Many times what is learned in an exercise is overlooked if it is not explicitly stated. Dr. Sidney B. Simon suggests that students make what he calls "I learned . . ." statements. After each activity, ask the students to record what they have learned *about themselves* in the form of "I learned . . ." statements:

I learned that I . . .

I relearned that I . . .

I was surprised to find that I . . .

I reaffirmed that I . . .

These can be included in the students' journals sometimes and on other occasions worked into a class discussion

We have found it useful when working with students in the affective domain to precede and follow each activity with a "here and now wheel." Ask the students to draw a circle with four lines intersecting in it at right angles (see below). On the lines have the students write one word that describes how they are feeling right now (i.e., happy, sad, tired, frustrated, anxious, relaxed, angry, loving, stupid, foolish, confident, etc.). Then ask them to choose one of the four words and expand it into two sentences. For example, "I feel happy because Sally picked me to be her partner. I didn't know she liked me."

Having the students compare their wheels before and after an exercise helps them see how their feelings about themselves change during an activity.

It is the cumulative effect over a long period of time that makes the journal effective. As it evolves into a very complete book about the student, it will become a precious document to her.

I am happy that I have such a nice teacher.

I am curious about self-esteem.

I am puzzled because I don't understand Africa.

I am satisfied with my work.

> Mr. Jacobs won our hearts, because he treated us as though we were already what we could only hope to become. Through his eyes we saw ourselves as capable and decent and destined for greatness. He gave direction to our longings and left us with the conviction that our fate can be forged by our hopes and deeds; that our lives need not be shaped by accident; that our happiness does not depend upon happenstance. Mr. Jacobs introduced us to ourselves. We learned who we were and what we wanted to be. No longer strangers to ourselves, we felt at home in the world.
>
> —An unnamed student
> quoted in *Teacher and Child*
> by Dr. Haim Ginott

that's the story of my life!

Writing an autobiography is a good exercise for juniors and seniors in high school, especially for an English class. One way to approach such an effort is to break the task into smaller components. The exercises that appear below can all be done as individual writing assignments in preparation for writing an autobiography. These assignments can be written in individual journals.

1. Ask students to write an autobiography of their hair. It is to be written as if their hair were the author. They should describe all the major events and changes in their lives as their hair.

2. Have the students draw the floor plans of the last two apartments or houses they have lived in. When they have completed their drawings, ask them to form into groups of three. Ask them to take the other members of their group on a guided tour through one of their houses, describing all the rooms, the furniture in them, where they used to play, study, hide, watch TV, sleep, eat, daydream, etc. When working with college students or teacher trainees, have them draw floor plans of their elementary or high school.

3. Ask the students to list who their heroes or heroines were when they were in elementary and junior high schools. Who were the bullies in their neighborhood? Who were their friends? How did they feel about them?

4. Who has been most influential in shaping their lives to date? Have some been better than others?

5. Have them write about the special events of their lives—both good and bad. How did they affect them when they occurred? How do they affect them now?

6. Ask students to describe their best friend. Pay attention to their friend's personality and character. How do they interact?

7. With older students, ask them to list and describe each of the major turning points in their lives.

> Self-esteem is the disposition to experience oneself as competent to cope with the challenges of life and as deserving of happiness.
> —Nathaniel Branden
> quoted in *Student Self-Esteem: A Vital Element of School Success*

3 autobiographical questionnaires

The autobiographic questionnaire is another tool to help a student expand his perception of himself. Looked at from semester to semester, the questionnaire can be an important instrument in helping someone enhance his self-concept.

At the beginning of each semester and again at the end of the year, the students should be asked to fill out the questionnaire. Having the students review their answers at the end of the year is a very illuminating experience in the quest for answers to the question "Who am I?"

Listed below are some sample questions for an autobiographical questionnaire. You should feel free to delete, add, or adapt questions from this list in order to fit your particular needs.

1. Name

2. Birth date   Age in years

3. Address   Phone number

4. List ten words that best describe you.

5. List ten words that best describe each person in your family.

6. What do you see yourself doing five years from now? Ten years from now? Twenty?

7. How do you spend your time after school and on weekends?

8. Of all the things you do in your free time, which do you like the most? The least?

9. Without mentioning specific names, what are the qualities of adults you respect and admire the most? The least? What are you doing to become more like the former? To keep from being like the latter?

10. Who is your best friend? What do your friends have in common?

11. What are your favorite sports, hobbies, or crafts, if any?

12. What are your favorite TV shows?

13. What magazines do you enjoy reading regularly?

14. What is there about you that makes your friends like you?

15. What major goals are you working on right now?

16. What does friendship mean to you?

17. What do you think of school?

18. Are you content with yourself? Would you like to be better? Would you like help and advice in this respect?

19. What value has life for you?

20. How do you spend your free time?

Adapted from Sidney B. Simon

A child's life is like a piece of paper on which every passerby leaves a mark.
Ancient Chinese proverb

A TRUE STORY

A preschooler named Maximillian was sitting in class smiling broadly. The teacher watched for a moment, then gently asked what he was smiling about.

"Just think," Maximillian said, motioning with his arm, "Some day this will all be mine!"

Ann C. Wells

"I have blue eyes and dark brown hair. I have some freckles, not many though. I have a small nose. I have regular size ears. I have medium size hair."

Lawrence Branagan and Christopher Moroney

28

4 ten questions

This is a variation of the old standard, "Twenty Questions." In this exercise, the students first write down a list of personal characteristics that are *positive* about themselves. The list can include physical characteristics, skills, hobbies, or interests, but should definitely include personality and character traits.

Tell students to keep their private lists with them as they form groups of three or four. When the groups are together, have members count off as one, two, three, and four.

The number one person starts by saying, "You have ten questions to guess which of my 'positive qualities' [or "characteristics," or "things about myself," or "virtues," depending on the age and maturity of the participants] I am pointing to on my list." The group then takes turns trying to guess what the quality might be. Be sure to emphasize that both the characteristics and the guesses must be positive.

When a group member offers a guess, the focus person responds by saying, "Yes, thank you, I am *honest, a generous person, etc.,* but that's not the one I'm pointing to," or until the correct answer is given, when she says, "Yes, thank you, that's it. I'm *a good ball player.*"

When ten questions have been exhausted or when the quality has been guessed, the next person takes a turn. Thus, each student gets bombarded with qualities that classmates find positive about her.

With younger children, you may have to precede this game by placing on the board a long list of class-generated qualities that might be used in this game.

Dr. Lillian Stover Wells

We in education may have overemphasized what can and should be done *for* and *to* students and have clearly not given enough emphasis to what can be done *with* and *by* students.

Garry R. Walz and Jeanne C. Bleuer
Student Self-Esteem: A Vital Element of School Success

5 collage of self

Instruct your students to make a collage entitled "Me!" Provide each student with a 12 × 18-inch sheet of thick construction paper or thin cardboard. They should collect and cut out pictures, words, and symbols that are representative of themselves—things they like to do, things they own, things they would like to own, places they've been, people they admire, etc. Then they are to paste these pictures, words, and symbols onto their sheets of construction paper to make a collage. Instruct the students not to sign them.

After the individual collages are completed, display them in the classroom. First, have the students try to guess who made each collage. Next have each student explain to the class all the items in his collage. Note for the class that the collages are all somewhat different—unique—just as each person, while having much in common with all others, is a different and unique individual.

You will probably need several class periods to complete this project. Try to have a lot of magazines with pictures available for the students. Magazines such as *Ms.*, *Ebony*, *Black Sports*, *Women in Sports*, *Auto World*, etc., should be included. The greater the variety of magazines, the better.

> The great law of culture is to let each one become all that he was created capable of being; expand, if possible, to his full growth; and show himself at length in his own shape and stature, be these what they may.
>
> Thomas Carlyle

6 the name game

This two-part exercise has several learning goals. It can be used to help students learn each other's names and to establish positive feelings of the students toward themselves and toward their classmates. In the event that the students are already well acquainted, start with Part Two.

1. The class sits in a circle. The teacher starts by saying, "I am Miss Jones." The first student to her right says, "I am Billy and that's Miss Jones." This process is continued around the circle until the last person has repeated everybody's name.

2. The second time around, each person must add something he is good at in addition to name. For example, "I am singing Miss Jones." "I am basketball-playing Billy and that's singing Miss Jones." "I am mountain-climbing Sally and that's basketball-playing Billy and that's singing Miss Jones." And so on around the circle.

3. Another variation is to have each person add an adjective that describes how she is feeling at the moment. For example, "I'm happy Miss Jones." "I'm tired Billy and that's happy Miss Jones." "I'm angry Sally and that's tired Billy and that's happy Miss Jones."

In all things we learn only from those we love. Goethe	The teacher gives not of his wisdom, But rather of his faith and lovingness. Kahlil Gibran The Prophet

7 my values bank

Have each student bring in a shoebox or similar container that can be kept handy in the classroom. These can be decorated with shelf paper or photographs or individual creative efforts so that each container can be easily identified.

Share with your class the two lists of values on pages 49 and 50 as you explain why being aware of one's own values is important. Note that people act on their values all the time, often without being conscious of them. For example, most students want to succeed at something—that is, they value success. They also, we hope, value education, as does American society—that's why we have free compulsory education.

Post a list of values in a prominent place in the classroom to help students become aware of values they may not have thought about.

Now, after discussing these ideas, explain how to use the Values Savings Bank. Have some Values Savings Deposit slips prepared. Distribute one to each class member, and keep the rest available for easy access at student initiative.

The Bank is where a student deposits a record of when and how he or she acted on some value held dear.

Here is a sample Values Savings Deposit slip:

VALUES SAVINGS DEPOSIT*

Deposit one outstanding example of my values in action:

_____
the value

_____
action taken

_____   _____
date   signature

* This deposit can be withdrawn and redeposited as often as desired for satisfaction, pride, joy, and self-esteem.

When an individual stands up to peer pressure, for instance, that student might want to save the incident in the Values Savings Bank, by describing very briefly the incident and perhaps labeling the value *courage*. Later it can be withdrawn for rereading and the taking of satisfaction anew in a courageous performance in light of personal values.

An extension of this values emphasis would be to enlist the support of your school principal and faculty in promoting a "Value of the Month."

This exercise takes "values" out of the nebulous arena of conversation and philosophy and brings them alive in practical and concrete experience.

Ann C. Wells

autobiographical sharing

In order for the child's self-concept to grow, he needs to be in an environment of trust and support so that he can feel secure enough to take risks. One of the best methods for developing an environment of trust is mutual self-disclosure.

Ask the students to sit in a circle. Tell them that each of them will have a specific amount of time in which to give an autobiographical sketch. Appoint one student with a second hand on his watch to be the timer. If you're working with elementary students, you may have to supply the watch. When working with a small group of eight to ten students, you may wish to use a three-minute egg timer.

Ask the students to share those important experiences throughout their lives, beginning with early childhood, which they consider of importance in the sense of leaving a strong impression on their personalities.

In this type of exercise it is a good idea for you to be the first one to share in order to model the behavior you want from the students. This also creates an environment of less risk. After you have shared, you may want to flip a coin to decide whether to proceed clockwise or counterclockwise around the circle.

After sharing the autobiographical sketches, you can ask the students if they would like to go around again and share things they remembered as the others were talking. Perhaps you or the students would like to suggest other areas for sharing. One fourth-grade class we worked with decided that they wanted to share accounts of their past physical injuries.

As you facilitate the sharing, take advantage of opportunities to point out commonalities in the experiences of the students: "Wow, we sure have a lot of ex–Girl Scouts in this group, don't we?" "Gee, Mario! Did you and O.J. know that you both played drums?"

Adapted from Herbert A. Otto

> Joy is the feeling that comes from the fulfillment of one's potential. Fulfillment brings to an individual the feeling that he can cope with his environment; the sense of confidence in himself as a significant, competent, lovable person who is capable of handling situations as they arise, able to use fully his own capacities, and free to express his feelings.
>
> William C. Schutz
> *Joy*

9 getting to know you

Getting to know another person can be an exciting adventure. One of the most important aspects of getting to know another person is the exchange of information. In fact, one of the causes of problems in relationships is the simple lack of information. When you don't know something about someone, you tend to fill in the vacuum with assumptions, fantasies, and unrealistic expectations. As we begin to know another person, it is important to get some of our "who" and "why" and "what" questions answered.

We have listed below a series of questions that can be used in several different ways. Students can be asked to pick a partner and answer some or all of these questions. You could give them the entire list on a duplicated sheet, write it on the blackboard, or just use a few of the questions. You can also have students pick a partner, answer one or two questions chosen by you, and then pick another partner, and so on. This way each person gets to know a little more about a lot of other people. You could also use these questions in small groups of four to six students.

The questions listed below work best with teenagers and adults.

1. How would your parents have described you as a child (age 6 to 12)?

2. What was your favorite toy as a child?

3. What is your favorite toy now?

4. What were you most proud of as a child?

5. What was your childhood nickname and how did you feel about it?

6. Do you like your first name now? If not, what would you like instead?

7. What is your favorite possession?

8. Can you name a favorite possession you no longer possess, and describe your feelings about no longer having it?

9. What is the funniest thing that ever happened to you?

10. What is the silliest thing you have ever done?

11. What is the stupidest thing you have ever done?

12. What is your all-time favorite movie? Why does it have special meaning for you?

13. What is your favorite book? What in it has personal meaning for you?

14. With what fictional hero or heroine do you most closely identify?

15. How good a friend are you? Give an example.

16. With what member of your family do you most identify? Why?

17. If you had to be someone else instead of yourself, whom would you choose? Why?

18. Who is your best friend of the same sex?

19. Who is your best friend of the opposite sex?

20. What do you look for most in a friend?

21. Name something you hate to do. What do you hate about it?

22. What in life is most important to you?

23. What do you like most about this class?

24. What do you like least about this class?

25. How would you change this class to make it better?

Adapted from the work of Jerry Gillies

The secret of education lies in respecting the pupil.

Ralph Waldo Emerson
The Complete Works of Ralph Waldo Emerson

---

10 success recall

Guided visualization is a technique that is extremely useful and has become increasingly popular in recent years in various kinds of learning situations. This particular visualization is easy, fun, and nonthreatening. A good warm-up for the next activity—Success Sharing.

Ask the students to close their eyes. Suggest that they take several deep breaths to relax and become comfortable. Ask them to imagine that there is a motion picture screen in front of their eyes and that they can recall their past and project it onto the screen.

Have them think back to a really happy day when they were between six and ten years of age. Ask them to see themselves waking up in the bedroom they slept in at that time. Can they remember whether they had a single, twin, bunk bed, or couch? Did they share the room with anyone? The bed? Ask them to look around the room and see the other furniture. Where were their toys kept? Was their a window? Did they have breakfast first, go to the bathroom, wash up, play with their pet, or what? Ask them to imagine a typical day—their school, their playmates, their playground, etc.

Ask them, with their eyes still closed, to begin to focus on a success they had during that period of their life. Can they remember one? Where did it take place? Did they do it alone? Did they plan for it or did it happen spontaneously? Can they remember how it felt when they completed the achievement? Can they recreate those feelings in their bodies now? Did they tell anyone about the success? Whom? Can they remember that experience? How did that person, or those people, react? etc.

Have them open their eyes and share their success experiences with a partner or small group.

> One of the main things his [Dr. Charles Garfield's] research showed was that almost all of the world-class athletes and other peak performers are visualizers. They see it; they feel it; they experience it before they actually do it. They begin with the end in mind.
>
> Stephen R. Covey
> *The Seven Habits of Highly Effective People*

DENNIS THE MENACE

"THE SECRET, JOEY, IS TO KNOW YOU'RE SOMEBODY WITHOUT *THINKING* YOU'RE SOMEBODY."

11 success sharing

Another way to help students focus on the postive aspects of themselves is to have them publicly share their accomplishments with the group.

In small groups of five or six, or with the entire class, ask the students to share a success, accomplishment, or achievement they had before they were ten years old. Next ask them to share a success they had between the ages of ten and fifteen; then between the age of fifteen and the present time. (Obviously, these age ranges will need to be revised depending on the ages of the students in your class.)

At first some students may have difficulty remembering some of their earlier successes, but as others share theirs, they will recall their own. Children with extremely low self-concepts often report that they haven't had any successes. If this happens, you will need to help prod the students with questions such as:

> Well, you've been taking care of your younger brothers and sisters for two years; I consider that an accomplishment!

> Can you remember when you learned to ride your bicycle? Did you feel good about that achievement?

One way to enrich the effect of this exercise is to precede it with the Success Recall (see Exercise 10).

A variation of this exercise is to periodically ask your students to share their greatest success or accomplishment during a recent period of time—say, the past week, the last month, over the weekend, over vacation break, over the summer, etc. It is also a good practice at the end of each day to ask the students what their greatest success was for the day.

. . . over time, a continuing and steadfast focus on the positive in life, on our strengths, and on the strengths of others can help to restore in our students their personal energy, their feelings of power, their sense of worth so that they can see themselves as positive forces who can contribute to the task of building a better world.

Robert C. Hawley
Human Values in the Classroom

---

12 the magic box

This is an excellent exercise for elementary school children.

Construct a "magic box" which can be any kind of a box with a mirror placed so as to reflect the face of anyone who looks inside. Begin the activity by asking the class, "Who do you think is the most special person in the whole world?" After allowing the children to respond with their individual answers, you may then continue, "Well, I have a magic box with me today, and each of you will have a chance to look inside and discover the most important person in the world."

Give each child a chance to look into the box after you ask them who they think they will see. Some children may have to be coaxed, because they may not believe what they see. Be ready with some of the following comments: "Are you surprised?" "How does it feel to see that you are the special person?" "You smiled so big—like you're happy to see that you're the special person." Before rejoining the class, ask each child to keep the special news a secret.

After all the children have had their turns, ask the group who the most special person was. After each child has had an opportunity to say "me," explain that the box is valuable because it shows that each of them is a special person. You might then want to ask how it is possible for everyone to be the special one. A discussion about each individual's uniqueness may ensue.

Suggested by Marlowe Berg, California State University at San Diego,
and Patricia Wolleat, University of Wisconsin

Whenever a value is set forth which can only be attained by a few, the conditions are ripe for widespread feelings of personal inadequacy. An outstanding example In American society is the fierce competitiveness of the school system. No educational system in the world has so many examinations, or so emphasizes grades, as the American school system. Children are constantly being ranked and evaluated. The superior achievement of one child tends to debase the achievement of another.

Morris Rosenberg
Society and the Adolescent Self-Image

13 hotshots

In the primary grades, set up a bulletin board as a class newspaper, with a name something like "The Room Four Brag." Use large sheets of lined newsprint. To begin each day, ask students to provide headlines about events or their own accomplishments that are newsworthy—that is, achievements that others may not know of, in which they take pride. Print a few headlines each day, or have children do so, and use these as leads for writing exercises.

In middle or junior high school, prepare duplicated sheets with the heading "TODAY I AM PROUD OF" in large type and the dates of school days for two weeks at the beginning of each of ten double lines. To begin the school day, ask students to take five minutes to jot an event of accomplishment unknown to the rest of the class. At the end of each week, provide a time for small group exchange of *the most important* of the five items listed. Ask students to link these events or incidents with values important to them.

During the course of the school year, repeat this exercise from time to time.

Dr. Kathleen M. Kies

14 values sharing

Our self-esteem is enhanced to the extent that we are clear about what our values are and that we act in accordance with them. The pressures for students to behave in ways contrary to their own beliefs is pretty awesome. For example, an individual may believe that courage is important but may bow to peer pressure without recognizing that courage in the face of what peers suggest is the test of that value.

Dr. Milton Rokeach has been a pioneer researcher on human values. This exercise is based on his excellent work.

On page 49 is Professor Rokeach's list of Instrumental Values—that is, those values that help us achieve our goals. His Terminal Values, sometimes called "End States of Existence," follow on page 50.

Give each student a copy of the Values Survey and have students rank-order the values from 1 (their top value) through 18 (the value they'd rank as least important in their lives).

When they complete their rankings, have them get into groups of four or five and share their rankings and the reasons behind their rankings. Give each student two to three minutes to discuss his or her list.

Afterwards, you may wish to conduct a full class discussion. Be prepared: The students may want you to share your rankings, so make sure you do yours as well. If they ask, be sure you advise them that your values do not necessarily represent the "right" ranking—but simply your way of looking at these issues.

Junior/middle school and high school students may wish to take a clean Values Survey home and ask their parents to rank-order their values. The class can then tabulate their class rankings and compare them with the parents' rankings.[1]

This comparison of rankings could be extended to include an entire class or the whole school, with discussion about the reasons for similarities and differences.

You may want to keep student rankings over a period of years to see if value changes are occurring.

---

[1] Select two or three students to do the tabulation. Have them record on a Values Survey sheet the rank number that each participant gave that particular value. Total the scores for each value. The fewer total points scored by a value, the higher the ranking by that group.

A TRUE STORY

The preschool children were to be interviewed by public school personnel to determine their readiness for entering kindergarten. There was some trepidation in the group, but the most concerned seemed to be Cathy, who actually was quite advanced and ready for whatever might come.

Nevertheless, to reassure her, her teacher took her on her lap and, holding her, said, "Cathy, you're going to do so well in kindergarten. You are great at recess, you use your body very well, your math skills are terrific, you can count to 100, and your reading is excellent. You know all of your letters!"

Cathy popped out of her teacher's arms, and looking her straight in the eye with her hands on her hips, said, "Well, it makes me believe I'm just marvelous!"

Ann C. Wells

VALUES SURVEY—INSTRUMENTAL VALUES

Below is a list of 18 values arranged in alphabetical order. Your task is to arrange them in order of their importance to YOU, as guiding principles in YOUR life.

    Study the list carefully. Then place a 1 next to the value which is most important for you , place a 2 next to the value which is second most important to you, etc. The value which is least important, relative to the others, should be ranked 18 .

    Work slowly and think carefully. If you change your mind, feel free to change your answers. The end result should truly show how you really feel.

_____ AMBITIOUS (hard-working, aspiring)

_____ BROADMINDED (open-minded)

_____ CAPABLE (competent, effective)

_____ CHEERFUL (lighthearted, joyful)

_____ CLEAN (neat, tidy)

_____ COURAGEOUS (standing up for your beliefs)

_____ FORGIVING (willing to pardon others)

_____ HELPFUL (working for the welfare of others)

_____ HONEST (sincere, truthful)

_____ IMAGINATIVE (daring, creative)

_____ INDEPENDENT (self-reliant, self-sufficient)

_____ INTELLECTUAL (intelligent, reflective)

_____ LOGICAL (consistent, rational)

_____ LOVING (affectionate, tender)

_____ OBEDIENT (dutiful, respectful)

_____ POLITE (courteous, well-mannered)

_____ RESPONSIBLE (dependable, reliable)

_____ SELF-CONTROLLED (restrained, self-disciplined)

VALUES SURVEY—TERMINAL VALUES

Below is a list of 18 values arranged in alphabetical order. Your task is to arrange them in order of their importance to YOU, as guiding principles in YOUR life.

Study the list carefully. Then place a 1 next to the value which is most important for you , place a 2 next to the value which is second most important to you, etc. The value which is least important, relative to the others, should be ranked 18 .

Work slowly and think carefully. If you change your mind, feel free to change your answers. The end result should truly show how you really feel.

_____ A COMFORTABLE LIFE (a prosperous life)

_____ AN EXCITING LIFE (a stimulating, active life)

_____ A SENSE OF ACCOMPLISHMENT (lasting contribution)

_____ A WORLD AT PEACE (free of war and conflict)

_____ A WORLD OF BEAUTY (beauty of nature and the arts)

_____ EQUALITY (brotherhood, equal opportunity for all)

_____ FAMILY SECURITY (taking care of loved ones)

_____ FREEDOM (independence, free choice)

_____ HAPPINESS (contentedness)

_____ INNER HARMONY (freedom from inner conflict)

_____ MATURE LOVE (sexual and spiritual intimacy)

_____ NATIONAL SECURITY (protection from attack)

_____ PLEASURE (an enjoyable, leisurely life)

_____ SALVATION (saved, eternal life)

_____ SELF-RESPECT (self-esteem)

_____ SOCIAL RECOGNITION (respect, admiration)

_____ TRUE FRIENDSHIP (close companionship)

_____ WISDOM (a mature understanding of life)

15 pride line

Pride is related to self-concept. People enjoy expressing pride in something they've done that might have gone unrecognized otherwise. Our culture does not encourage such expressions and it is sometimes difficult for people to actually say, "I'm proud that I . . ."

Ask each student to make a statement about a specific area of behavior, beginning with, "I'm proud that I . . ." For example, you might say, "I'd like you to mention something about your *letter writing* that you're proud of. Please begin your response with 'I am proud that I . . .'" Students may pass if they wish.

Below are some suggested items for use in this exercise.

1. Things you've done for your parents
2. Things you've done for a friend
3. Work in school
4. How you spend your free time
5. About your religious beliefs
6. How you've earned some money
7. Something you've bought recently
8. How you usually spend your money
9. Habits you have
10. Something you do often
11. What you are proudest of in your life
12. Something you have shared
13. Something you tried hard for
14. Something you own
15. Thoughts about people who are different from you
16. Something you've done in regard to ecology
17. Something you've done in regard to racism
18. Something you've done or do anonymously

We learned this exercise from our friend Sid Simon.

Self love, my liege, is not so vile a sin as self neglecting.

Shakespeare
King Henry V, act II, scene 4

WHAT IS A NATIVE AMERICAN?

*A native American is a group of people made up
        of many tribes and cultures.
We are a people of laughter and sadness
        a people of remembrance and anger.
We are a people of sight and beauty
        a people of wisdom and knowledge.
We are a people of honor and respect
        a people of prayer and thankfulness.
We are a people that are one with Mother Earth
        and she provides for us.
We are artistic with the days now gone, and we are
        poetic with the sounds of the winds and cries
        of the past.
We are a people that survived for centuries when
        the world around us wanted us dead.
We are a people that are in the minds of the others,
        that wish we were a memory of long ago.
We are a people of healers and prophecy.
We are a people of mystery and awe.
We are brothers and sisters to the animal world around us.
We are the thunder and the lightning; we are the hail and
        snow or a reed in the wind.
I have met all these people in my travels, and of the
        others that want to be of the people, they may
        come close, but they cannot totally because they
        do not possess certain qualities that we are born with.
We are a unique and beautiful people.
We are the Native Americans.*

WA-SHEA-KWU (Lynette Shawano), Wisconsin

16 success a day

At the end of each day, have the students briefly share with the rest of the class the successes they have experienced during that day.

Some students will find this difficult at first, but as others begin to share, they too will realize they have had some of the same successes. It has been our experience that if a student says he has had no success, some of his classmates will chime in with successes they have seen him accomplish. The sensitive teacher will also look for successes to be pointed out to the child with extremely low self-esteem.

A variation of this activity is to have each child share with the class what he feels he has learned that day. In addition to being a great form of review, it provides the student with a sense of accomplishment. Without recall, students are often not consciously aware of all the learning they are accomplishing in and out of school each day. Knowing that he is learning adds positively to a child's self-concept.

If you are trying to build writing skills, have the students write a paragraph recording their successes rather then reporting them verbally. This method also leaves an accumulated record which the student can review at the end of the week.

> True, all children need to experience their competence to build self-respect. But each child needs to feel that his person is cherished regardless of his competence. Successful performances build the sense of worthwhileness; being cherished as a person nurtures the feeling of being loved. Every child needs to feel *both* loved and worthwhile. But *lovability must not be tied to worthwhile performance.* The more lovable any child feels, however, the more likely he is to perform in satisfactory ways, for then he likes himself.
>
> Dorothy Corkille Briggs
> *Your Child's Self-Esteem*

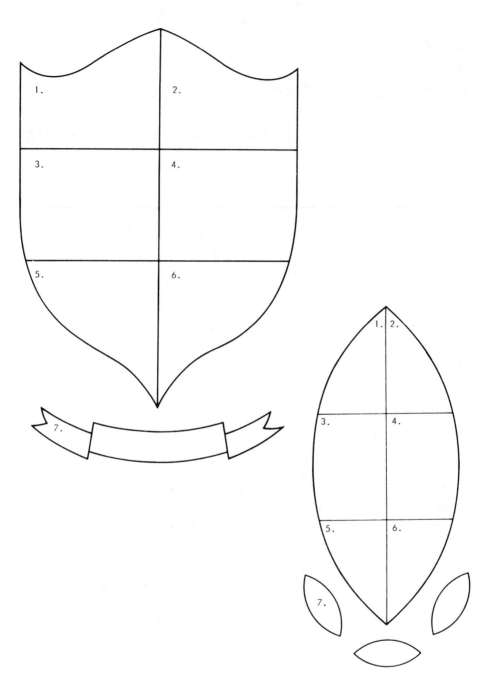

In working with African-American students you may wish to use a "coat-of-arms" shaped like an African war shield such as that illustrated on the right, rather than a shield derived from European heraldry such as the one illustrated above. When teaching an integrated class, we suggest offering both options.

17 personal coat-of-arms

This exercise is a way of combining several self-enhancing questions with some art work and small group disclosure.

Photocopy sheets with the design that appears on the opposite page and distribute it to the students. Ask each of them to create an individual coat of arms by making a drawing in the appropriate section expressing their thoughts regarding each of the following questions:

1. Express in a drawing the most significant event in your life from birth to age fourteen.

2. Express in a drawing the most significant event in your life from age fourteen to the present.

3. Express in a drawing your greatest success or achievement in the past year.

4. Express in a drawing your happiest moment in the past year.

5. If you had one year to live and were guaranteed success in whatever you attempted, what would you attempt? Draw a picture expressing your answer.

6. Express in a drawing something you are good at.

7. If you died today, what three words would you most like to be said of you?

Any number of questions could be substituted for those above in order to adapt the exercise to different age levels. Some optional questions for drawings are:

1. What is something you are striving to become or be?
2. What is your family's greatest achievement?
3. What would you want to accomplish by the time your are sixty-five?
4. Draw a picture of something you'd like to become better at.

When the drawings are completed, ask the students to form groups of five or six and share what they have done with the small group. When they have finished sharing, you may wish to post all the coats-of-arms on a bulletin board or wall for a day or two.

After the students have shared their drawings in the small groups, you may wish to have them make several "I learned . . ." statements in their journals.

Suggested by Sister Louise, St. Juliana's School, Chicago, Illinois

Totem Pole

This figure shows a totem pole coat-of-arms, which can be used with Native Americans.

18 personal flag

The teacher begins this activity by holding up a symbol (e.g., the peace symbol) and asks if anyone knows what it is. She or he may then respond with, "Yes, it is a peace symbol. It's a popular symbol that many people recognize. I have some other symbols with me also. Look at this one and see if you can tell what it means." The teacher may then hold up a dollar sign, for example. "Here are some other symbols [mathematical symbols, traffic symbols, etc.] that you probably see every day. Can you think of others?"

The teacher should then explain that a symbol is a picture or design that stands for something, just as the peace symbol represents the idea of peace. "People make symbols. Someone makes up a symbol and the rest of us learn what it means. Let's see if we can make up some of our own." The children can then work as a group in making up symbols for such concepts as happiness, spring, sadness, family, sports, etc.

The teacher may then show a picture of an American flag and explain that a flag is another kind of symbol and consists of many parts. "Does anyone know what the stars stand for? the stripes? the colors? Every country has a flag and the different parts of the flag stand for something that is important to the people. Today you are going to make your own *personal* flags, and make symbols for things about you."

The personal flag may be used as a way of identifying symbols of feeling toward a variety of people and situations—e.g., friendship, school, careers, special moments, values, habits, life goals, etc.

After the children have completed their drawings, the teacher can then lead a discussion in which the students are asked to share the meanings of their symbols with the rest of the class if they wish. At this point it is important for the teacher to keep in mind that it is not his or her task to give advice to the children, but rather to show interest and understanding and reflect on the value and meaning of their symbolized experiences.

Suggested by Marlowe Berg and Patricia Wolleat

There are only two lasting bequests we can hope to give our children. One of these is roots; the other, wings.

Hodding Carter

19 ball of yarn

A student at Eastern Michigan University taught us this interesting exercise.

She led us outside to a lovely, shaded lawn area (although this exercise could be done inside). She had us form a large circle, shoulder to shoulder.

We then gently tossed a large, continuous ball of purple yarn around the circle to form a colorful web. With each toss, we called out the name of the person we were throwing to and said something we admired about the receiver.

When we finished, we went back to the classroom to *generalize* about our experience.

Some of our generalizations and personal insights may be similar to what you'll get from your group:

- We are all connected.
- We can create beautiful things if we work together.
- It is very pleasant to hear someone unexpected say nice things about you.
- It is more fun to work together than to work alone.
- The joy on people's faces as they were complimented made me happy as well.
- I felt I was with a special group of people.

> The ultimate freedom is the right to choose my attitude in any given situation.
> Victor Frankl
> *Man's Search for Meaning*

20 self-portrait

This is a good initial activity for any age level. The self-portrait can be easily and effectively executed as a sketch, drawing or painting in a wide variety of art media, such as chalk, pencil, ink, charcoal, crayon, pastel, water color or tempera. Length of the activity will be largely determined by age level and the particular medium selected.

Self-portraits may be created impromptu from memory or from mirrors. Be accepting and encouraging during the pupil's first try; wait a few weeks—then try again. It is helpful if you work along with the class on a portrait of yourself. In fact, teacher participation is suggested for all of the activities in this book.

Create occasions for displaying the self-portraits frequently. Birthdays and special projects provide ideal opportunities for using portraits. Try using signed portraits in place of name tags to identify individual students' projects and papers.

From James J. Foley

Oliver Wendell Holmes once attended a meeting in which he was the shortest man present.
"Doctor Holmes," quipped a friend, "I should think you'd feel rather small among us big fellows."
"I do," retorted Holmes, "I feel like a dime among a lot of pennies."

Note: The best book we've seen on helping young people draw better is Mona Brookes, *Drawing with children.* Los Angeles: Jeremy P. Tarcher, 1986.

Rubes®   By Leigh Rubin

If cows had agents.

21 success symbols

All of us have symbols of success—things that remind us of our past successes. We have photographs, medals, certificates, dried-up corsages, dance books, ticket stubs, autographed baseballs, newspaper clippings, poetry, bronzed shoes, trophies, plaques, ribbons, and mounted golf balls, fish, and antlers. Most of us save these objects because they remind us of our abilities and competencies and our likability and popularity.

Have the students bring to class five tangible objects that recall or symbolize some past successes or accomplishments they have had.

During the next class period have each student share one or more of his "success symbols" with the rest of the class. Instruct the students to share the feelings and meaning connected with the specific object as well as the success it symbolizes.

A variation of the success symbol concept is to have the students list five success symbols they do not have but would like to acquire in the next year, five years, etc. This activity could be used in conjunction with goal-setting. Be sure to discuss the choices or goals without judgment; be open to whatever the students come up with.

As a teacher, what are your success symbols? Take a walk through your house or apartment and see how many are visible. If they are all stored away in drawers and closets, consider how you might make them a more *integral* part of your environment.

Suggested by Herbert Otto

A first-grader proudly showed his mother the gold star he had earned in school. "We get these for what we do best," he explained. "And what do you do best?" she asked. "I'm the best rester!" beamed the boy.

Everyone wants to be good at something. And most of us are. Young, old, or middle-aged, we all have a built-in drive to excel.

22 what's my bag?

Here's a fun activity for any age. It is a combination of Exercises 20 and 21.

Have your group collect a large number of success symbols and other meaningful objects that represent who they are and place them in a shopping bag.

Next, have them decorate the outside of the shopping bag with personally related pictures, words, and symbols, thus producing a three-dimensional collage.

This exercise can also be done using a cigar box or any other kind of container.

Another wonderful grocery bag exercise is to declare Local Self-Esteem Week in your community. Ask a local grocery chain to donate two bags per student for your entire school. Make sure one side has no printing on it.

Ask the students to complete the following two statements, and then illustrate them in crayon—one in each bag.

1. I am proud that I. . .
2. I feel good about myself because . . .

When the bags are completed, they are returned to the grocery store and used for people's groceries on Self-Esteem Day. If you are in a small enough community, you can even get local newspaper coverage, complete with photos of sample bags.

One school district we know got the whole district involved and distributed over 6,000 bags.

Suggested by Sandy Holland

The child must first learn self-respect and a sense of dignity that grows out of his increasing self-understanding before he can learn to respect the personalities and rights and differences of others.

Virginia M. Axline
Dibs: In Search of Self

FEELINGS LIST

abandoned	fearful	passive
accepted	flexible	passionate
afraid	foolish	peaceful
agile	free	pessimistic
annoyed	frustrated	phony
anxious	funny	playful
angry	furious	pleased
ashamed	fulfilled	pressured
		protective
bad	gentle	productive
balanced	glad	puzzled
believable	glum	
bewildered	good	rejected
bitter	grateful	relieved
bold	guilty	resentful
bored		restless
brave	happy	
brilliant	hated	sad
	high	selfish
calculating	hopeful	sensual
calm	hostile	sentimental
calloused	humiliated	sexy
cold	hurt	showy
concerned		shy
confident	inadequate	silly
confused	inhibited	strong
cunning	intense	
curious	intimidated	tender
	irritable	tense
defeated		terrified
defensive	jaded	tired
delighted	jazzed	tough
depressed	jealous	trapped
desperate	joyful	
detached		ugly
disappointed	limited	uneasy
disgusted	lonely	uptight
distant	loose	used
distinguished	loving	useless
disturbed		
dreary	macho	vibrant
	mean	victorious
eager	miserable	vulnerable
edgy	mistreated	
elated		wanted
elegant	needed	warm
embarrassed	neglected	weak
enthusiastic	nervous	wonderful
envious		worried
ecstatic	optimistic	
excited	overloaded	youthful

23 becoming aware of feelings

This is the first of several lessons to help students become aware of and cope with their feelings. It is most suitable for *primary grade children.*

At the beginning of the day, ask the children what they know about emotions. As the children talk, they should come to understand that *emotions* and *feelings* are roughly the same. As the children discuss feelings, list those mentioned on the board. You may get such responses as:

sad	happy	excited
scared	eager	daring
angry	proud	surprised
nervous	loving	puzzled

(See page 68 for an extended list of feelings.)

Have each child make a chart with words we use for feelings, listing the words in a column at the left and setting up two or three columns on the right for entries of times. As their feelings change throughout the day, students can be asked to record the time when they are experiencing a particular emotion. For example, something might happen at 9:30 that would stimulate a feeling of anger. The individual should record the time in the first column beside *angry* on his or her chart. If anger occurs frequently, use of all three columns might indicate a need for individual exploration of causes with a particular child.

Late in the afternoon you may wish to have a class discussion about the feelings recorded during the day. You may want to ask how many felt sad at some time, how many felt happy, bored, or nervous.

You may wish to discover whether a particular emotion was recorded at a relatively common time. Discussion might reveal, for example, that something you said or did made the children feel happy, or that a particular behavior of one group had an effect on the emotions of all the students. This kind of discussion will help the class see that there is a link, not necessarily causal, between the behavior of people in their environment and their own feelings. Other aspects of this discussion might stem from questions such as:

1. What did you do about the feeling you had?

2. How did you express that feeling?

3. If you were happy, did you smile?

4. If you were sad, did you cry?

5. What caused you to be angry? . . . excited? . . . happy?

6. Did you tell the person *who may have caused it* that you were angry? How did you express your anger? At this age, children think others are responsible for their feelings. In the discussion, begin to point out that others do not make them happy, sad, or angry; that *how they think about what others say or do to them determines how they feel.* This is a hard concept, even for some adults, so don't belabor the point. They'll have more opportunities to grasp the idea as they mature.

You can conclude this discussion of feelings by pointing out the purpose of this lesson—that is, that conscious awareness of feelings is the first step in helping one to cope with his or her damaging or negative feelings. If the children have enjoyed doing this, you may want to repeat the experience several times during the year.

A great follow-up is the next activity—One-way Feeling Glasses.

> Nothing is as beautiful as a laughing child.
>
> Harold Clive Wells

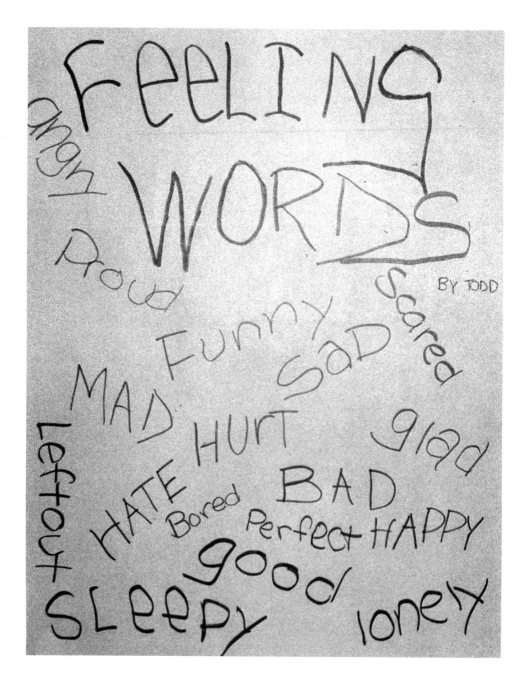

24 one-way feeling glasses

Our friend Gerry Weinstein developed this exercise and it's a good one. As the group leader, explain that you have some "magic glasses" for their eyes. You hold out your hands and "show" them, although they're invisible! (You might use inexpensive eyeglass frames.) Let each participant pretend to take a pair of glasses out of your hands and put them on. Then ask if they notice that these magic glasses enable them to see everything "through happy eyes." Everything looks nice, joyous—the world is a happy place. Have them interact on that basis.

When you think they're ready for a change, help them switch their glasses to "angry glasses." Now the world is an angry place. Everything that's done causes angry responses. The room is full of grouches. Again, let them interact for a while.

At an appropriate time you may switch to other glasses such as:

Scared	Gloomy	Suspicious	Stubborn
Bragging	Things are O.K.	Modest	
Nobody loves me	Curious	Show-off	

After several role-playing situations, carry on a discussion of their feeling while wearing different types of glasses. Have there been days when they think you've had on a particular pair of one-way feeling glasses? Do they know people who seem to always wear one type of glasses? Probe for what the exercise may mean to them in their own daily behavior. See if they can begin to realize that they have control over their emotions. They can choose to put on more satisfying glasses.

From Gerald Weinstein and Mario Fantini

> The aim was to have each student realize that restricting himself to a single view of people and situations limited his power, identity, and relations with others, and that if he could, through practice, learn to see some situations in new ways, he might find these to be more satisfying, potent, and useful than the old.
>
> Gerald Weinstein and Mario Fantini
> *Toward Humanistic Education*

By GARY LARSON

"Bummer of a birthmark, Hal."

25 meaningful symbols

Divide a blackboard or sheet of newsprint into as many sections as there are students and then ask each student to draw a symbol or picture of something that is meaningful to him—something he is concerned about, that he likes, dislikes, hates, or loves.

One by one, ask each student to explain his drawing and to tell the class why it has meaning for her.

This seemingly simple exercise has a great impact on students. In peer-group situations students seldom have an opportunity to talk about the things that concern them. In addition to discovering that other people share some of the same deep concerns, the student will experience the ideas, feelings, and thoughts of others as being worthwhile and important; she will thus begin to believe in herself as more worthwhile and important also.

Adapted from the Self-Enhancing Education Project

> A person learns significantly only those things which he perceives as being involved in the maintenance of, or enhancement of, the structure of self.
> Carl R. Rogers
> *Perceiving, Behaving, and Becoming*

26 object sharing

This activity is suitable for any age group, from preschool to adult.

Begin by bringing in an object that has special significance to you and sharing it by saying something like this: "I would like to share something with you that gives me a good feeling."

Explain why the object is meaningful to you—for example: "Here's a necklace that someone I like very much gave to me. Whenever I wear it I am reminded of that person, and that makes me feel cared for. I would like to give you a chance to share something with us and tell us why it makes you feel the way you do. So, please bring an object that is meaningful to you to class tomorrow so that you can share it with us."

When you reconvene, give students an opportunity to share their objects in small groups or with the whole class. Sometimes this can take place over several days as participants bring sentimental objects from home.

27 those nasty put-downs

Ugly remarks and nicknames directed at a child by siblings or peers is one of the most damaging and persistent occurrences of childhood. There may not be a young person anywhere who has not felt the sting of another's remarks. Often these are bigoted attacks, but anyone who is seen as too thin, too fat, too tall, too short, too light, too dark, too smart, too dumb, too annoying, or in any way different has had this unfortunate and often devastating experience.

This exercise teaches young people how to defuse or cope with this all-too-common ugliness and thus preserve their self-esteem. The key ideas in handling attacks are:

1. Assertively take a position on your own behalf.
2. Do it without hostility.

For many years we've taught students to say,

NO MATTER WHAT YOU SAY OR DO TO ME,

I AM STILL A WORTHWHILE PERSON!

Have your class copy this from the board several times. It can be repeated aloud by the students in response to the teacher's good-natured insults. (Students love to do this—see Activity 28.

Having this response thoroughly internalized by members of your class will help them for years to come.

In sharing this exercise with a group of teachers, we were told about a child who had suffered disfigurement from burns. This boy had learned through painful experience that he had to have a response ready that would be nonattacking and yet preserve his self-concept. What he learned to say in an objective, matter-of-fact way was:

> *If you knew the pain I've suffered and the courage it takes for me to be here, you wouldn't say such things to me. Thanks a lot.*

And he would turn and walk away.

Dr. Louise Hart, in her book, *The Winning Family*, describes a friend who gets up each morning and "waxes his back." His strategy is to take preventive measures by metaphorically waxing his back so that whatever negativity may fall on him that day will wash right off, just as the oily feathers protect a duck. Great idea!

American gymnast Betty Okino was on the U.S. Olympic team in 1992. When she was asked how it felt to be one of two blacks on the team, she wisely responded: "I came to compete for my country, not for any certain race—black or white. I consider myself an American, not a color."

you can quote me on this!

No matter what you say or do to me, I'm still a worthwhile person!

Ask the students to close their eyes and repeat in unison with you the chant: **"No matter what you say or do to me, I'm still a worthwhile person!"**

This seemingly simple exercise has a very powerful impact if done repeatedly. It implants a new seed thought in each of the students; it acts as an antidote to all the negative thoughts and statements already implanted in their thinking.

A way to heighten the effect of this exercise is to ask students to imagine the face of someone who has put them down in some way in the past—a parent, teacher, coach, friend, fellow student, Girl Scout leader, policeman, etc.—each time they begin to say, "No matter . . ." Have them stick out their chins, smile, and repeat the sentence strongly, with conviction. After they get the hang of it, you should interject statements like, "You're stupid, you're ugly, I hate you, you're a retard, Hi, Chubby, here comes brace face, freckleface, you're fired, you're not wanted here," etc., and let them respond to these with, **"No matter what you say or do to me, I'm still a worthwhile person."**

Please repeat this exercise for twenty-one school days. There is now research that indicates that it takes twenty-one days to change a mental habit.

> The most deadly of all sins is the mutilation of a child's spirit.
>
> Erik H. Erikson
> *Young Man Luther*

FRANK & ERNEST® by Bob Thaves

29 dear me letter

It is important for the student to be able to integrate and find meaning in his experiences. A "Dear Me" letter at the end of an exercise or a class can serve this purpose. It can also serve as an effective means of ongoing evaluation for the teacher.

Ask each student to individually take time to integrate her experience by writing a letter to herself. You can suggest questions or statements to facilitate the writing, such as:

> What was the high point of the session?
> What was the low point?
> I learned that I . . .
> I felt . . .
> I relearned . . .
> What was unique about your response?
> What was typical of your behavior?
> How honest were you when you were sharing?
> What about your behavior did you like the most?
> What about your behavior did you like the least?
> I need . . .
> I am concerned about . . .
> I wonder . . .
> This class would have been better if only . . .
> If only I . . .
> I appreciated myself for . . .

These letters can be written in the journals, or they can be handed in to the teacher. To do both, have the students use a piece of carbon paper. The original stays in the journal; the carbon is handed in to you. Students who wish to keep some of their responses private might remove the carbon paper while recording these responses.

Contributed by Joel Goodman

Self-expression leads to growth and expanded awareness. Those who stifle themselves for fear of criticism "pay the piper in dis-ease and the stunted growth of personality and psyche. Those who express themselves unfold in health, beauty and human potential. They become unblocked channels through which creativity, intuition and inspiration can flow.

Christopher Hills and Robert B. Stone
Conduct Your Own Awareness Session

30 re-entry questions

During the first few weeks of working in small groups, it is a good idea to open each session with a re-entry question. These questions are designed to re-establish the level of group rapport that has been developed, as well as to positively enhance the self-concepts of the participants.

Some of the following suggestions have been described in earlier portions of this book. You may find them fun to do again or simply skip over them, perhaps saving them for a later date. Here are some useful re-entry questions.

What is the most exciting thing that has happened to you in the last week? Over the weekend? Yesterday? What is the most exciting thing you did?

Suppose you have a magic box; it can be any size or shape. In it can be anything you want that would make you happy. What is in your box that makes you extremely happy?

Suppose a doctor had just told you that you have only one year left to live. What would you do differently? How would you change your life? (This exercise can be used in conjunction with goal-setting. For example, "What is stopping you from doing some of these things now? Let's set a goal to achieve some of those things.") Suppose you only had one hour to live, starting right now—what would you do?

Share with the group an experience in which you made someone happy. In which someone made you happy.

If you could teach everybody in the world just one thing—an idea, a skill, a precept, a fact—what would it be?

What would you say has been the greatest learning experience of your life? Of the past week?

If you could be talented in something you are not talented in now, what would it be? Is it something that would please you? please others?

86

31 accurate listening—for content and feelings

Begin this important activity *for upper elementary and high school levels* by asking students to write down three things that are bothering them. These can be personal (the best) or perhaps something at school or in world events, as long as they're genuinely concerned about them.

Ask for a volunteer to be interviewed by you in front of the class. When you're both seated, ask the student to choose one of the three concerns and begin to talk about it.

As she does, reflect back to her in your own words what you heard her say. For example:

> *Student:* I'm upset about the use of drugs in our society and I wish the government would do more to stop it!

> *Teacher* (paraphrasing): You think our government is not attacking the drug problem forcibly enough.

> *Student:* Yes, it seems like we can spend money on everything, like other countries or our military, but not enough on social problems here at home.

> *Teacher:* Not enough governmental funds are given to solving problems like drugs, homelessness, and other social problems.

Stop after two or three paraphrases and point out what you are doing. Say that you want the speaker to be sure she feels properly heard. If she does, you proceed. If not, you ask for clarification and paraphrase until the speaker is satisfied that she's been heard.

This paraphrasing skill is the best way we've found to teach people to listen. It requires a great deal of energy to do it correctly, and it should be used selectively. The rewards are great, however. The listener should elect to use paraphrasing whenever the speaker has a high investment in what she's saying.

The second, and more difficult, aspect of this exercise is to listen and respond to the emotional content of the speaker's message.

While working with the same volunteer, begin to focus on her feelings and reflect them back to her as she talks. For example:

> *Student:* It seems stupid to me that drugs continue to be imported into our country from all over the globe!

Teacher: You seem pretty *angry* about that!

Student: Of course. Why can't the peacetime military be used to stop it?

Teacher: It's pretty *frustrating* to you that no one seems to be preventing the importation of drugs into our community.

Again, stop and tell the class what you're doing. Recognize that this sounds somewhat phony at times, but the listening skill involved takes practice to learn. It's kind of like a first baseman throwing easy ground balls to infielders between innings.

Dr. Haim Ginott has pointed out that when a person is experiencing a strong emotion, you should respond to him in such a way as to recognize his *feelings* first, before dealing with the event or the cause.

This skill of reflecting back the speaker's feelings is also one that must be used selectively—when the speaker is feeling an emotion intensely. However, practice can occur in the more structured setting you are providing.

After this demonstration, break your group into clusters of three. Designate one person in each triad as a speaker (person with a problem, selected from her three concerns written earlier), the second person as the listener, and the third as an observer. The observer may take notes but not talk until asked to do so.

Give the speaker and listener about five minutes to talk and practice paraphrasing. After five minutes, stop them and have them rotate roles so that each person has an opportunity to play all three roles. At the conclusion of each five-minute period, the observer tells what she heard—that is, instances of successful and unsuccessful listening (paraphrasing).

Discuss this experience for a few minutes and then repeat the exercise with the added instructions to reflect the speaker's feelings as well as the content or message she is conveying.

This activity may be one of the most difficult in this book, but it is worth the effort because of its powerful impact on relationships.

Adults have a lot of trouble with it, too, yet we all agree that listening is of vital importance in human interactions and that we generally don't do it very well.

Please continue to have your students practice these skills throughout the year until they master them.

We are always equal to what we undertake with resolution.

Thomas Jefferson

32 an academic strategy

All the exercises in this book are expected to help students acquire academic competence. The ability to function successfully in the classroom is critical to a young person's self-esteem, and, as we pointed out earlier, there is a reciprocal relationship between self-esteem and academic competence—each supports and enhances the other. Some of our exercises, like the Perfect Student Visualization, Incredible Affirmations, and this one, are targeted more directly than the others at successful learning.

We've had particular success with this strategy in teaching reading (letter and word recognition and phonics), spelling, and geography, but it has other applications as well.

In general, we've used this selectively with people from the primary grades through adulthood who feel they can't succeed in these skills or subjects.

For a student who constantly fails or is less than mediocre in spelling, we begin by asking her what is the most difficult word she can think of. We generally get *encyclopedia*. We then take a sheet of paper and a crayon and spell out *en/cy/clo/ ped/i/a* slowly, saying each syllable (or sound break) in the word as we write it. The student then rehearses, slowly spelling out the word *syllable* by *syllable* while running her index finger over the raised crayon surface as she writes it. She is instructed *not* to say the letters, only the *sounds* of the syllables as she traces them.

When she has done that several times correctly, looking at the correct crayoned spelling, cover it and have her write it while sounding it out, just as she has been seeing and tracing it. She'll get it right 90 percent of the time. If she misses, however, she goes back to saying the syllables as she traces them about five times. Then she can repeat the blind spelling correctly.

Spelling lists can be attacked in this way with phenomenal success if the student is willing to practice patiently. We've seen students go from "F" grades to "A"s and "B"s almost overnight, with a resultant boost to their morale and self-esteem.

To learn letters or words or phonetic sounds or draw maps, the same technique is used. That is, a correct example is given with a raised surface—some teachers have used fine sandpaper—that can be traced with one's fingers. The combination of seeing, feeling, and speaking simultaneously is what ingrains the material in the student's brain.

Because one-on-one time is difficult for teachers to manage, it is recommended that you teach this method to an aide or other students who can supervise and encourage the struggling student's practice.

THE FAR SIDE

By GARY LARSON

Primitive spelling bees

33 verbal martial arts

You can use this exercise with anyone or any group from about the age of ten to adulthood. This strategy is an extension of Exercise 29, which deals with the self-esteem maintenance task of handling insults—something everyone is familiar with but not necessarily skilled in dealing with.

We use a four quadrant diagram formed by drawing two sets of polar positions: *active/passive* and *constructive/destructive*. Each quadrant is then appropriately labeled:

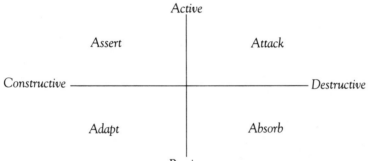

1. *Attack (Active/Destructive)*: Responding by attacking back, calling the other person names, hitting, getting even. This mode respects the responder's feelings/rights but not the original attacker's. Examples:

"I might be fat, but you're a skinny jerk."
"Oh, yeah? You're just stupid."

Say: "I'm going to teach you a model today to help you understand how people usually react to putdowns and how you can respond to them. You will learn ways that will make you feel better about yourself rather than worse."

Now draw the model on the board and explain the four quadrants. (Additional help in understanding this model may be obtained by studying Exercise 102 on page 255.)

Give examples as shown above of each way of reacting to insults. With the class, go over each of the putdowns you've written on the board and ask for examples of responses in each quadrant, being sure the students understand the meaning of the terms used.

See if they can figure out some additional *assert* (assertive) responses.

Finally, explain how each type of response to a putdown can affect their feelings of self-esteem and that of the other person.

- *Active/destructive* responses respect the rights of the insulter but not the responder.

- *Active/constructive* responses are best because they preserve the self-esteem of the responder and yet do not violate the insulter's rights.

- *Passive/destructive* responses respect the insulter's rights but damage the self-esteem of the recipient.

- *Passive/constructive* responses minimally protect the self-respect and rights of the responder while protecting the insulter.

End this lesson by having the class copy and discuss their interpersonal rights.

MY INTERPERSONAL RIGHTS

1. The right to be treated with respect.
2. The right to have and express feelings.
3. The right to my own opinion.
4. The right to say "no."
5. The right to make mistakes.
6. The right to feel good about myself.

If you haven't the courage to be the hammer, you'll be in the role of the anvil.

Oswald Spengler

WORDS THAT ENCOURAGE
Dr. William Halton

- Everybody makes mistakes.
- You are the kind who can do it.
- Failure is no crime.
- You are improving.
- Mistakes do happen.
- I like the way you are listening.
- You try it. You can do it.
- That is very nice work.
- Thanks so very much.
- That is really great.
- I appreciate your considerate behavior.
- Keep up your good work.
- It's so nice to know someone like you.
- What a neat idea.
- Your work is really improving.
- I feel so good inside when you work so nicely together.
- Bravo! You got _____.
- I'm very proud to be your teacher.
- Your help is really appreciated.
- _____ is really getting down to work.
- Let's show the entire class your story.
- Please, read your ideas to everyone.
- That's an excellent idea.
- You make that really look easy.
- When you do nice things for each other, I get a very good feeling inside.
- It's marvelous to see everyone so alert.
- That was a very kind deed, work, etc.
- I could listen to you read, sign, etc., all day.
- I know, it's very hard.
- I understand how you must feel.
- I'm glad you are interested in _____.
- You're printing is very pretty.
- Good work.
- Nice going.
- Hard work does get results.
- That's great.
- Right on, brother.
- Your kindness is so refreshing.
- What a nice smile you have.
- I'm glad that you decided to try.

Mental Health Association of Tarrunt County
804 West 7th Street, Fort Worth, Texas 76102

34 positive reinforcement: an instructional solution

My first experience with positive reinforcement as a prevailing instructional technique occurred when I started my U.S. History course by giving everybody an "A." Or, to be more accurate, I gave everybody 600 points. Each week the students took a 40-point quiz. Exams were also given a predetermined number of points. Each quiz and exam was returned with the total number of points remaining to the student after I graded it. When their total dropped below 540, they had a "B." Below 500 they had a "C," etc. A funny thing happened that year. Nobody failed the course, with one exception by virtue of absences. Two sophomore students received the first "A" in their lives. Since they had seldom even earned a "B" in the previous thirteen years, I asked them how they were able to get an "A" all of a sudden. Their reply: this was the first time anybody had ever held out the hope of their getting an "A." They assumed it would be the last time, too. So they studied hard to keep it. I wonder what kind of students they would have been if their previous education had provided hope?

I adopted another simple technique of positive reinforcement: I gave away my red pencils. Think about it a moment: red symbolizes violence, blood, STOP, (immoral, godless) communism—a whole host of authoritarian, painful, paranoiac associations. On a student's paper it essentially means: "Here, stupid, is where you were stupid!" Red is negative reinforcement all the way. Editors have a reputation for being merciless, but even *they* use *blue* pencils.

The best system of positive reinforcement is, of course, to evaluate a student's work from the viewpoint of what is right with it rather than from that of what is wrong with it. Show the student what he has going for him. Point out his strengths. Show him how he can develop his strengths; that is, treat error in the context of nurturing capacity rather than as a process of revealing ignorance. The student already knows he's ignorant. That's the one thing they suceeded in teaching him before he got to you. Now he needs to know that he can do something about his ignorance.

The best way to affirm student performance via grading is to give grades only for that which can be affirmed. A number of junior colleges have adopted a grading system wherein no record is established in a course until the student has met the requirements for a passing grade. He can still fail a course (or courses), and thus suffer the attendant's loss of money, time, and effort, plus all the discouragement and disappointment that goes with it. That is, he still suffers the *consequences* of failure, but no punishment.

Negative grades are, after all, primarily punitive. Sort of like fining a fellow $500 for being broke.

Noel McInnis

 **quickies**

1. *Do Well:* Sitting in a circle, ask the children to share with the group something they like to do and that they do well.

2. *Pen Pal:* Ask the students to write a letter describing themselves to an imaginary pen pal. Encourage them to go beyond mere physical descriptions, adding things like hobbies, family composition, favorite subjects, etc.

3. *My Body:* Ask the students to consider the following: What are the beautiful parts of your body? The ugliest? Where did you get your notions of beauty? How do TV commercials affect your notion of beauty? How does your body influence yourself? What are bodies for, anyway?

4. *My Assets:* Ask students to write a paragraph about themselves describing the assets they have, the negative traits they would like to eliminate, and the positive characteristics they would like to obtain or develop. In dealing with the negative aspects, it is important to distinguish between things that can be changed (a bad disposition) and things that cannot be changed (a weak chin).

5. *Puppets:* Ask a group of elementary students to work alone or together to make up a story about themselves. Then have them make hand puppets representing the characters and to act out the story they have written. Encourage them to focus on the positive qualities of the participants.

6. *Self-Worth:* Have the students write a story about something they can do to make other people feel worthy or happy.

7. *Get Well:* When a student is sick for an extended period of time, initiate a class project to make or buy a gift for the sick child. One class we know of constructed a giant "We miss you!" card from individual paintings done by the children. The effect of caring and giving is as powerful on the class as is the effect of receiving and being cared for on the child who is ill.

8. *Class Mural:* Tape a long sheet of butcher paper to the wall, provide the class with lots of crayons, and ask the students to draw a "class mural" depicting the things they do in common and the things they do that are more uniquely their own.

9. *Classroom or School Newspaper:* The creation of a classroom newspaper is a good way to provide children with the opportunity to see their names and

their work in print. Articles can also be written about the children's achievements. Recognition, in print, of positive services, activities, and achievements does a lot to increase and improve self-concept. Students can select the name of the paper, choose editors and reporters, conduct interviews, and draw illustrations. On a school basis, each room could have a reporter, who might change from time to time, to collect and gather material for publication. The writing of the newspaper also helps strengthen written language skills. The newspaper could also be used in various classrooms for reading instruction.

10. *Write a Story:* Ask the students to write a story about themselves as "neat" people. Specifically instruct them to deal with personality and character—what they like about the way they are. In other words, discourage them from thinking of themselves as only their talents, skills, or achievements, but rather their feelings, thoughts, and behaviors.

11. *The Nicest Thing Ever:* Have the whole class write *The Nicest Thing Ever* book. Let each child write and illustrate two contributions:
    (a) The Nicest Thing I Ever Did for Anyone" (ask them to explain what it was, why they did it, and how it made them feel).
    (b) "The Nicest Thing Anyone Ever Did for Me" (ask them to describe it, why they think someone did it, and how it made a difference in what might have happened).
    (c) "The Nicest Thing I Ever Did for Myself."

12. *Teaching:* Ask students to share with the class one area in which they feel confident enough to teach another person. This could be a hobby, a skill, a sport, a musical instrument, a special interest, etc. Also, ask them what they would like to learn if someone in the class had the skill to teach them.

13. *Breaking a Record:* Ask students what record they would break if they could break any record in the world. Why would they do it?

14. *I Can:* Ask the students to write a story about a boy or girl who faces a physical test of courage and resourcefulness and succeeds; or a story about a teenager who suddenly finds himself in trouble and gets out of it.

15. *Graffiti Board:* Get some butcher paper or newsprint and designate an area where kids can write or draw anything they want. It's their place to let off steam in a nondestructive way. Periodically place new paper over the old so that new graffiti can be collected.

two

my strengths

We've maintained that the most effective way to enhance a person's capacity to develop her full potential is to concentrate on her strengths. Negativism and "attacking" procedures seem to us to be inappropriate, especially in the school setting.

You'll find the activities in this section interesting. It is unfortunate but true that many youngsters feel that they have no strengths—just as you have probably found that they had a hard time acknowledging pride and successes in the previous section. To some extent this is a manifestation of our cultural emphasis on humility. In our society it is not usually deemed "proper" to indicate pride or pleasure at one's successes and strengths. That's too bad. We'd like to see people secure in the knowledge that they can do many things well. In fact, a "can do" attitude is one we wish teachers would continuously foster. Obviously, some people cover up a deep sense of "I'm *not* O.K." by blustering, bragging behavior. These people, too, need a firmer conviction of their real strengths. "The 'I Can't' Funeral" is a delight and the "Strength Bombardment" exercise always has a significant impact on participants.

> Good teachers know that discomfort and pain are often signs that truth is struggling to be born among us.
>
> Parker J. Palmer
> *To Know as We Are Known*

THE ANIMAL SCHOOL:
The Administration of the School Curriculum
with References to Individual Differences
Dr. George H. Reavis

Once upon a time, the animals decided they must do something heroic to meet the problems of "a new world." So they organized a school.

They adopted an activity curriculum consisting of running, climbing, swimming, and flying. To make it easier to administer the curriculum *all* the animals took *all* the subjects.

The duck was excellent in swimming, in fact better than his instructor; but he made only passing grades in flying and was very poor in running. Since he was slow in running, he had to stay after school and also drop swimming in order to practice running. This was kept up until his feet were badly worn and he was only average in swimming. *But average was acceptable in school so nobody worried about that except the duck.*

The rabbit started at the top of the class in running, but had a nervous breakdown because of so much make-up work in swimming.

The squirrel was excellent in climbing until he developed frustration in the flying class where his teacher made him start from the ground up instead of from the tree top down. He also developed a "charliehorse" from overexertion and then got C in climbing and D in running.

The eagle was a problem child and was disciplined severely. In the climbing class he beat all the others to the top of the tree, but insisted on using his own way to get there.

At the end of the year, an abnormal eel that could swim exceedingly well, and also run, climb, and fly a little, had the highest average and was valedictorian.

The prairie dogs stayed out of school and fought the tax levy because the administration would not add digging and burrowing to the curriculum. They apprenticed their children to a badger and later joined the groundhogs and gophers to start a successful private school.

Does this fable have a moral?

36 IALAC

The IALAC Story is told to illustrate how one's self-concept can be destroyed by others. If done with feeling and imagination, it can be a very powerful and moving experience. We have found that it is appropriate for students of all ages.

Take a sheet of paper and write the letters IALAC (pronounced "I-ah-lack") on it in large bold print. Holding this to your chest so that the students can see it, tell them, "Everyone carries an invisible IALAC sign around with them at all times and wherever they go. IALAC stands for 'I am lovable and capable.' This is our self-concept, or how we feel about ourselves. The size of our sign—or how good we feel about ourselves—is often affected by how others interact with us. If somebody is nasty to us, teases us, or puts us down, rejects us, hits us, etc., then a piece of our IALAC sign is destroyed. [Illustrate this by tearing a corner piece off the sign.] I am going to tell you a story to illustrate how this happens in everyday life." Then proceed to tell the students about a boy or girl who is the same age they are. Pick a name that no one in the class has. As you tell the story, try to be as emotional and dramatic as you can without burlesquing it too much. An outline is provided below. You will have to fill it in with your own imagination. Some teachers we know have the children help create the story as you go along. As you describe each event that negatively affects the student's IALAC sign, tear another piece of the sign off until at the end you are left with almost nothing.

A possible outline for the IALAC story is as follows. Feel free to adapt, add to, change, and embellish it in any way you want.

A seventh-grade boy named Michael is still lying in bed three minutes after his alarm goes off. All of a sudden, his mother calls to him, "Michael, you lazy-head, get your body out of bed and get down here before I send your father up there!" (rip!) Michael gets out of bed, goes to get dressed, and can't find a clean pair of socks. His mother tells him he'll have to wear yesterday's pair. (rip!) He goes to brush his teeth and his older sister, who's already locked herself in the bathroom, tells him to drop dead! (rip!) He goes to breakfast and finds soggy cereal waiting for him. (rip!) As he leaves for school, he forgets his lunch and his mother calls to him, "Michael you've forgotten your lunch; you'd forget your head if it weren't attached!" (rip!) As he gets to the corner, he sees the school bus pull away and so he has to walk to school. (rip!) He's late to school and has to get a pass from the principal, who gives him a lecture. (rip!)

Continue the story through the school day with appropriate examples. Some possibilities are:

Forgetting his homework

Getting a 68 on a spelling test

Being called on for the only homework question he can't answer

Making a mistake in reading so that all the kids laugh

Being picked last to play ball at recess

Dropping his tray in the lunchroom, with everybody applauding

Being picked on by bullies on the way home from school

Being referred to as "Hey you!" in gym class

You can think of other examples or get the students to help you.

When Michael gets home from school some typical negative events might include not being able to watch the baseball game because his father is watching his favorite TV show or because he has not yet finished his homework, or being told to wash the dishes for the third night in a row because his older brother has band practice, etc.

End the story by showing Michael going to bed with an IALAC sign about as big as a quarter! When you finish, ask the kids to discuss the following questions:

How does *your* IALAC sign get torn up? What things affect you the most?

What do you do that destroys the IALAC signs of others—in school, family, etc.?

How do you feel when your IALAC sign is ripped? When you rip someone else's?

What can we do to help people enlarge their signs rather than make them smaller?

This exercise can also be used in conjunction with Exercise 29—"Nasty Putdowns." In the exercises that follow, activities are presented that help students paste their own and others' IALAC signs back together again. Exercise 30—"You Can Quote Me on This!"—can also be used in relation to IALAC, with the idea that whenever someone tries to rip your IALAC sign, you can simply repeat the "No matter what you say or do to me, I'm still a worthwhile person."

One class we know of spent a whole week wearing IALAC signs and actually ripping them apart anytime someone said or did something damaging to their self-concept. Whenever a sign was ripped, the class had to stop and discuss what had just happened. The learning that took place was incredible. Several teachers have enthusiastically reported trying this with their families. Have fun with it. It is a powerful technique. See Exercise 57 for a later follow-up.

The IALAC story was originally conceived by Sidney Simon and Merrill Harmin. Simon has written and published the story for use by students and teachers. For a copy, write Argus Communications, 7440 Natchez Avenue, Niles, Illinois 60648.

Love and self-worth are so intertwined that they may properly be related through the use of the term identity. Thus we may say that the single basic need that people have is the requirement for an identity; the belief that we are someone in distinction to others, and that the someone is important and worthwhile. Then *love* and *self-worth may be considered the two pathways* that mankind has discovered that lead to a successful identity.

William Glasser, M.D.
Schools without Failure

37 personal evaluation sheet

The personal evaluation sheet is an informal, nonthreatening worksheet designed to help students clarify and verbalize their feelings about themselves in relation to everyday experiences. The evaluation sheet can be readily adapted to meet the requirements of a wide range of grade levels by alterations of the substance and structure of the questions.

The photocopied evaluation sheets are composed of sentence stubs or questions intended to stimulate responses about the concerns and attitudes shared by all children. Although the process itself is the primary objective of this activity, the feedback is often useful for future planning and follow-up.

Listed below are some suggested sentence stubs and questions that can be used on evaluation sheets. It is recommended that the number of questions be limited to ten or twelve. Questions may be deleted, added, or modified to fit classroom needs.

Today I feel very . . .	I enjoy reading about . . .
I enjoy . . .	I wish grownups would (wouldn't) . . .
I am unhappy when . . .	I like myself best when . . .
I feel good when . . .	If I had a choice, I would . . .
I wish my teacher(s) . . .	At school I am . . .
My classmates think I . . .	I wish . . .
School is . . .	Tomorrow I would like to . . .

With younger children it is sometimes useful to use questions that can be answered with "yes," "no," or "sometimes."

Do you like school? Your teacher? Your classmates?

Do you like yourself?

Are you a quiet person? A noisy person?

Are you an active person?

Are you usually happy? Unhappy?

Do you have many friends? A best friend?

Do you have fun at school? At home? Outside?

Did you like answering these question?

From James J. Foley

109

> There is no value judgment more important to man—no factor more decisive in his psychological development and motivation—than the estimate he passes on himself.
>
> Nathaniel Branden
> *The Psychology of Self-Esteem*

FRANK & ERNEST ® by Bob Thaves

strength bombardment

Have the students break into groups of five or six, preferably with other students they know well and feel comfortable with. Focusing on one person at a time, the group is to bombard him with all the strengths they see in him. The person being bombarded should remain silent until the group has finished. One member of the group should act as recorder, listing the strengths and giving them to the person when the group has finished. See the Personal Strengths sheets on pages 142 and 143 for stimulation of ideas.

The students should be instructed to list at least ten strengths for each student. They should also be cautioned that no "putdown" statements are allowed. Only positive assets are to be mentioned. At the end of the exercise, ask the students to discuss how they felt giving and receiving positive feedback. Was one easier than the other? Which one?

In some groups it is wise to spend ten minutes discussing with the class the different types of strengths that exist, as well as developing a vocabulary of strength words they can use. It may be a good thing to list all the words that are "brainstormed" on the chalkboard for the students to look at during the "bombardment" sessions.

To reinforce this activity, have your students also ask their parents to list the strengths they see in them. The new list could be added to that which is collected in class. This additional exercise will also provide the student with some very important positive feedback from parents.

Note to teachers: Haim Ginott in his book *Teacher and Child* makes the following useful distinction between evaluative feedback and appreciative feedback: Evaluative feedback is characterized by judgment—the teacher is the judge and the student is to be judged. Examples of this kind of feedback are: "*This* is a B− poem." "*You* are a good artist." "*You* are funny."

Appreciative feedback is characterized by letting the student know how you, as a person, have been affected by what they have done. Examples of appreciative feedback are: "*I* was deeply moved by your poem, *The Me I Never Dared to Be.*" As *I* read it *I* identified with the many fears you wrote about. *I* guess we are similar in more ways than *I* had imagined." "*I* enjoyed your pictures. *I* like the way you use colors to express motion and power." "*I* appreciate the way you are always able to relax the tension in the classroom with a joke or a story. *I* enjoy your humor."

Try as much as possible to use appreciative feedback with the students in both formal (papers, artwork, etc.) and informal (personal feedback, group discussions, etc.) situations. Try discussing this distinction with your students and encourage them to also use appreciative rather than evaluative feedback with each other. The key to the difference is that most evaluative feedback starts with the word *you;* most appreciative feedback starts with the word *I.*

We learned this activity from Herbert Otto.

Everything has its beauty but not everyone sees it.

Confucius

39 learning from failure

Begin by standing at the board ready to record in abbreviated form the student's responses. Indicate to the class that you want them to brainstorm for a few minutes. When you've explained the rules for brainstorming (all ideas valid, no discussion, everyone contributes an idea), state that the question is: "In what activities is it possible for you to have failure experiences?"

You'll probably get such responses as:

Fail at the end of the year	Fail to learn long division
Fail at sports	Fail in junior high school
Fail in high school	Can't learn to dance
Won't get married	Fail to get a job

When the class seems to have exhausted all the possible ideas, ask them to write down the three possible failures they worry most about, putting them in rank order with the thing they worry about most at the top of the list. The items listed in the brainstorming will help them recognize some of their own concerns. Tell them only you will see their list.

Now ask them to help you list behaviors exhibited by people who fail or are concerned about failure. You may get such responses as they:

act silly	eat too much	drink
might give up	act nervous	drop out
take drugs	stop trying	get angry
make excuses	pretend they don't care	
blame others	bully other people	

Point out to the students that not everyone who is afraid of failure acts like this, and nobody does *all* of these things. Remember, some people who are afraid of failure try harder; others compensate for failure in one area by being very successful in another.

Ask the students to go back to their own lists of three failure concerns. Ask them to write down their own most common reactions to failure or fear of failure. When they've done that, collect their papers. These will help you to understand each of your students better. You may choose to do some individual counseling on the basis of this idea. Continue this lesson by asking: "Do you think I'm a reasonably happy and successful person?" Most of your students will agree that you are, indeed. Explore with them the reasons they feel you are happy and successful.

For the final activity of this lesson, have the class sit in a tight circle with you for a discussion.

There is an assumption here that everyone has had some failure experiences in life. Youngsters, however, are often unaware of how others feel about such failures. To overcome this lack of awareness, please talk to the children about some failures in your own life. Do it seriously and with dignity and honesty. Discuss your feelings at the time of the experience and how you feel about it now. The class may want to ask you some questions.

In summary, ask: "What does all of this mean that we've talked about today?"

The students, after these brief experiences, should be able to come up with some excellent generalizations such as:

Everyone fails at something sometime.

It's OK to fail at something. It's not the end of your life.

If you persist, you *can* often overcome early failures.

You can learn (mature) from failure experiences.

Failure is only the opportunity to begin again more intelligently.

Henry Ford

The sense of obligation to continue is present in all of us.
A duty to strive is the duty of us all.
I felt a call to that duty.

—Abraham Lincoln

Probably the greatest example of persistence is Abraham Lincoln. If you want to learn about somebody who didn't quit, look no further.

Born into poverty, Lincoln was faced with defeat throughout his life. He lost eight elections, twice failed in business and suffered a nervous breakdown.

He could have quit many times—but he didn't and, because he didn't quit, he became one of the greatest presidents in the history of our country.

Lincoln was a champion and he never gave up. Here is a sketch of Lincoln's road to the White House:

1816	His family was forced out of their home. He had to work to support them.
1818	His mother died.
1831	Failed in business.
1832	Ran for state legislature—LOST.
1832	Also lost his job—wanted to go to law school but couldn't get in.
1833	Borrowed some money from a friend to begin a business and by the end of the year he was bankrupt. He spent the next seventeen years of his life paying off this debt.
1834	Ran for state legislature again—WON.
1835	Was engaged to be married, sweetheart died, and his heart was broken.
1836	Had a total nervous breakdown and was in bed for six months.
1838	Sought to become speaker of the state legislature—DEFEATED.
1840	Sought to become elector—DEFEATED.
1843	Ran for Congress—LOST.
1846	Ran for Congress again—THIS TIME HE WON—went to Washington and did a good job.
1848	Ran for reelection to Congress—LOST.
1849	Sought the job of land officer in his home state—REJECTED.
1854	Ran for U.S. Senate—LOST.
1856	Sought the vice-presidential nomination at his party's national convention—GOT FEWER THAN 100 VOTES.
1858	Ran for U.S. Senate again—AGAIN HE LOST.
1860	ELECTED PRESIDENT OF THE UNITED STATES.

The path was worn and slippery. My foot slipped from under me, knocking the other out of the way, but I recovered and said to myself, "It's a slip and not a fall."'

—Abraham Lincoln after losing a senate race

40 student of the week

Place the names of all your students in a box. Each week, in front of the class, draw one of the names from the box. The student whose name is drawn becomes the Student of the Week.

Ask the rest of the class to state the things they like about the chosen student. Be patient and encouraging; stress that everyone has many good qualities. You might also wish to tell the students that it is important to take this seriously because they too will one day have a turn. Try to get six to ten concrete statements listed. It is also a good idea to try to keep the lists equal in length.

Have the Student of the Week bring in a picture of himself, or take one of him with a Polaroid camera. Post his or her picture, name, and list of good qualities on the bulletin board. You may change this bulletin board each week, or you may wish to make a cumulative bulletin board of Students of the Week.

To ensure that all class members receive recognition within a shorter period of time, you may wish to have three students a week (Monday, Wednesday, Friday) or three on one day of the week.

Suggested by Astrid Collins

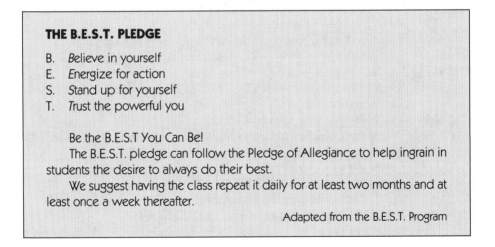

THE B.E.S.T. PLEDGE

B. *Believe in yourself*
E. *Energize for action*
S. *Stand up for yourself*
T. *Trust the powerful you*

Be the B.E.S.T You Can Be!
The B.E.S.T. pledge can follow the Pledge of Allegiance to help ingrain in students the desire to always do their best.
We suggest having the class repeat it daily for at least two months and at least once a week thereafter.

Adapted from the B.E.S.T. Program

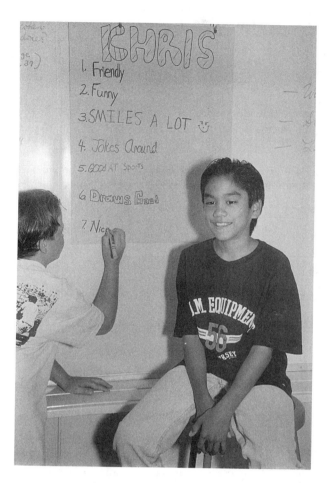

You see, really and truly, apart from the things anyone can pick up (the dressing and the proper way of speaking, and so on), the difference between a lady and a flower girl is not how she behaves, but how she's treated. I shall always be a flower girl to Professor Higgins, because he always treats me as a flower girl, and always will; but I know I can be a lady to you, because you always treat me as a lady, and always will.

Eliza Doolittle to Colonel Pickering
in George Bernard Shaw's *Pygmalion*

117

41 "I can't" funeral

One of the most exciting ideas we've run across is this one written by Chick Moorman about a Michigan teacher named Donna. (Unfortunately, we don't know her last name.)

The following excerpts will give you the idea. It's a great example of superior teaching, incorporating as it does cognitive, emotional, and kinesthetic learning.

The teacher began by instructing the students to make a list of all the things they could think of that they thought they couldn't do—their own list of "I can't"s. For example:

"I can't hit a home run over the fence."

"I can't do long division."

Donna, at the same time, wrote her list of "I can't"s: "I can't lose weight no matter how hard I try." And so on.

Several students filled an entire page with "I can't"s and proceeded with a second page. When the children had finished, Donna instructed them to fold their papers in half and bring them to the front of the room where she placed their "I can't" statements into an empty shoebox. When all of the students' papers were collected, Donna added hers. She put the lid on the box, tucked it under her arm and headed out the door and down the hall. The students followed the teacher.

Halfway down the hall the procession stopped. Donna entered the custodian's room, rummaged around, and came out with a shovel. Shovel in one hand, shoebox in the other, Donna marched the students out of the school to the farthest corner of the playground. There they began to dig.

They were going to bury their "I Can't"s! The digging took over ten minutes because most of the fourth graders wanted a turn. When the hole approached four feet deep, the digging ended. The box of "I Can't"s was placed in position at the bottom of the hole and quickly covered with dirt.

At this point, Donna announced, "Boys and girls, please join hands and bow your heads." The students complied. They quickly formed a circle around the grave,

This story is used by permission of the author from *Chicken Soup for the Soul: 101 Stories to Open the Heart and Rekindle the Spirit* by Jack Canfield and Mark Victor Hansen. Deerfield Beach, FL: Health Communications, 1993.

creating a bond with their hands. They lowered their heads and waited. Donna delivered the eulogy.

> *Friends, we gather today to honor the memory of "I Can't." While he was with us on earth, he touched the lives of everyone, some more than others. His name, unfortunately, has been spoken in every public building—schools, city halls, state capitols, and, yes, even the White House.*
>
> *We have provided "I Can't" with a final resting place and a headstone that contains his epitaph. He is survived by this brothers and sister, "I Can," "I Will," and "I'm Going to Right Away." They are not as well known as their famous relative and are certainly not as strong and powerful yet. Perhaps some day, with our help, they will make an even bigger mark on the world. May "I Can't" rest in peace, and may everyone present pick up their lives and move forward in his absence. Amen.*

At the conclusion of the eulogy, she turned the students around, marched them back into the classroom and held a wake.

They celebrated the passing of "I Can't" with cookies, popcorn, and fruit juices. As part of the celebration, Donna cut out a large tombstone from butcher paper. She wrote the words "I Can't" at the top and put RIP in the middle. The date was added at the bottom.

42 nicknames

Almost all children have nicknames. Some are complimentary; many are not! As part of our general orientation, we tend to discover each other's weaknesses, and in words like, Baldy, Fatso, Skinny, Rat, Sissy, Bull, Four-eyes, Dumbo, Ears, Slim, Worm, Stinky, and so on, exploit them.

Although these nicknames are often accepted by children, their effect on a developing self-concept is damaging. To reverse this trend have students give themselves and/or each other nicknames based on their strengths. For example, a good artist might be called Art; a horseshoe champ, Ringer or Champ; a basketball player, Wilt or Hoop; a physically strong boy, Bear; a person who likes gardening, Fleur, Violet, or Herb; a girl good in music, Melody.

Conduct a classroom discussion around the following questions: What are the names that would make you feel good—that would make you feel proud or self-confident? What are the names that make you feel bad—that make you lose your self-confidence? What would a classroom be like where everyone had a nickname that made him or her feel bad? What would a classroom be like if everyone had a nickname that made him feel good and self-confident?

Do you have any nicknames? How do they make you feel? What other names have you been called in your lifetime?

With older groups in high school you can have the class break into pairs. One at a time each student closes his eyes while his partner calls to him, repeatedly using one or more of his nicknames. Then the students can share the feelings evoked by the different names. These reactions should be recorded in their journals. This exercise can also be used as an introduction to writing poetry, short stories, etc.

A book entitled *The New Age Name Book* by Sue Browder (New York: Warner Paperback Library, 1974) contains over 3,000 unusual, symbolic, and creative names not found in usual name books. You might ask students to find a new name that means something special to them. Some examples of girls names are Solana (Spanish for "sunshine"), Shani (Swahili for "marvelous"), Cari (Turkish for "flowing like water"), Tara ("Buddhist savior goddess"), Shaina (Yiddish for "beautiful"). Shashi (Japanese for "bliss"), Chenoa (North American Indian name meaning "white dove"). Boys' names include Ari (Hebrew for "lion"), Erin (Irish for "peace"), Kem (English gypsy name meaning "the sun"), Krispin (Slovakian for "curly-haired"), Manco (Inca name meaning "king"), Yuma (American Indian name meaning "son of a chief"), Dustin (German for "a fighter"), and Ragnar (Swedish meaning "mighty army"). This book can also be used for the exercise.

Healthy people, research shows, see themselves as liked, wanted, acceptable, able and worthy. Not only do they feel that they are people of dignity and worth, but they behave as though they were. Indeed, it is in this factor of how a person sees himself that we are likely to find the most outstanding differences between high and low self-image people. It is not the people who feel that they are liked and wanted and acceptable and able who fill our prisons and mental hospitals. Rather it is those who feel deeply inadequate, unliked, unwanted, unacceptable, and unable.

Donald E. Hamachek
Encounter with the Self

43 what's in a name?

The purpose of this activity is to increase the student's self-concept through an understanding of his own names.

> What function do names serve? (They help us to identify and talk about specific individuals.)
>
> Who decides what name a person gets? (Parents)
>
> Where do parents get these names? (From their own names, from relatives, from books, from movies and television, from other people, etc.)

Names are passed down through history from one generation to another. At one time in history names actually had meanings. For example, first names like Philip meant "Lover of horses," Peter meant "rock or stone," Henry meant "home ruler," Edward meant "prosperous guardian," Margaret meant "a pearl," Judith meant "admired or praised," Ann (derived from Hannah) meant "full of grace, mercy, and prayer," and Shirley meant "from a white meadow."

Last names also had meaning. A "cooper" was a man who made barrels. A "smith" was a blacksmith, or one who worked with metal. A "miller" was one who ground grain, and a "potter" was a man who fashioned clay pottery.

Originally names were descriptive phrases to help identify people such as Philip, the cooper, or Peter, the smith. Eventually, the descriptive nouns came to stand for the people themselves—Philip Cooper and Peter Smith.

Using any of the readily available books of names, such as *6000 Names for Your Baby* (New York: Dell Publishing Company, 1983), allow the students to take turns looking up the meaning of their names and entering them in their journals. If a name is not listed, be sure to tell the student that it's because their name must be really special and suggest that they ask their parents for information on how their name was chosen or created.

Negative associations and images are often evoked by personal names. To combat this, youngsters can be taught to take pride in the names they've been given.

Susan Elizabeth Robles

44 going to Boston

This activity is a variation of an old memory game called "Going to Boston." In this variation, the first student says, "I'm going to Boston with my suitcase and in it I have my *smile* (here the student offers some characteristic or competency that is treasured). The next student then says, "I'm going to Boston and in my suitcase I have Juan's *smile* and my *skill at computer games.*" The third person says, "I'm going to Boston and in my suitcase I'm carrying *Juan's smile, Sally's skill at computer games,* and *my liking for other people.*" Continue until every group member has had an opportunity to insert a treasure.

Before beginning this game it might help to have each student pretend to "pack a suitcase" or trunk with self-perceived positive qualities and to draw a picture of the trunk with the qualities in it. Older students could symbolically represent the qualities with their drawings. For example, a heart represents love, a joystick could represent skill at computer games, and so on. You could ask them to discuss the following question: What is the biggest "item" in the trunk—that is, the most treasured quality?

Another variation: Pack the trunk with *successes.* Ask students to identify their biggest success to date. Teenagers can play the "Going to Boston" game using their successes. For example, I'm going to Boston with my suitcase and in it I have straight A's on may report card."

Dr. Lillian Stover Wells

It is as if you knew you were going to die tomorrow and you knew also that you could not make the transition if you left any people behind you that you hated. Imagine Heaven requiring love for everyone, no exceptions, and your having the capacity to make that happen. In many ways, heaven on earth does require exactly that—love that is not conditional, that is free from demands, that allows the loved one the right to be anything that he or she chooses without losing your love. This is the kind of surrendering that I am talking about, a kind of trust that everything is in perfect working order in the universe, including yourself.

Wayne D. Dyer
You'll See It When You Believe It

"I know that I am smart, as a matter of fact I am brilliant, I am great. In athletics the greatest, and the funny thing about this is that I am not conceited about it."

Lawrence Branagan and Christopher Moroney

45 commercial for oneself

Methods of selling products are hardly foreign to this generation, but how many have ever considered advertising their own strengths and skills? As a self-enhancing activity, tell the students they are going to spend the next several days making advertisements and commercials to sell themselves. They have the option of designing a magazine or newspaper advertisement, a poster, a billboard sign, a brochure, a radio or television commercial, or any other form of advertising they can think of (sweepstakes, coupons, etc.).

Allow several class periods for the students to develop their ideas and create their final product for display. You may wish to permit two or more students to work together in a team; for example, one student might be a good artist, another a good writer or photographer.

When students have completed their ads and commercials, take a period to share all of them with the entire class. We suggest that contests, judging, and prizes be avoided. They create unnecessary competition that can lead to feelings of inadequacy and resentment among those who do not win.

Materials needed: Poster paper, crayons, felt-tip pens, watercolors, brushes, scissors, magazines, newspapers, and paste. *If available:* computer, cassette recorder, CD or tape player, CDs or audiotapes, camcorder, VCR, 35mm cameras, etc.

> An optimist is wrong just about as often as a pessimist is, but the big difference is that he has a lot more fun.
>
> Anonymous

# 46 positive support techniques

Positive Feedback At the end of a small-group session, students often wish to give each other some feedback or other data about themselves. Some beginning statements for giving feedback in a positive manner include:

> I liked when you . . .   When you . . . I . . .
> It helped me when you . . . We were better as a group today because you . . .

Positive Support Ask each student to list, and later to share, five things that another person can say, do, or recognize in them that makes them feel good or successful. For example:

1. Smile when you see me
2. Listen to me when I talk
3. Tell me that my contribution was useful
4. Hug or kiss me to show affection
5. Tell me that you missed me while I was gone

Positive Support Sharing At some time during the week, suggest that the students make "I appreciate . . ." statements to each other. This can be done in the whole class, in small groups, or individually. This activity can encourage children to experiment, to take risks, and to try on new behaviors. It is important that you, as the teacher, model this "I appreciate . . ." behavior throughout the year. The exercise works best if you have each student share in turn around the room. This avoids the time delay and anxiety of waiting to see who goes next.

> There is a need of staggering magnitude for doing something in our educational program to help children and youth acquire realistic attitudes of self-acceptance. A large proportion of the young people now entering adulthood are burdened with anxiety, hostility, defensiveness, attitudes toward themselves and others, feelings of guilt, inferiority, or other forms of self-disparagement and self-distrust. They struggle not only with the real dangers and thwartings in our troubled world but with unresolved childhood problems. They are beset with conflicts arising from unrealistic concepts and unhealthy attitudes which they carry from childhood into adult life.
>
> Arthur T. Jersild
> *In Search of Self*

"Who am I and where am I going?"

three

who am I?

Ultimately, each of us is faced with three questions which we must answer in one way or another if we are to grow to greater personal maturity:

Who Am I?

Where Am I Going?

Why?

Each of these questions, in its own way, deals with our sense of self, our goals, our values, our strengths and weaknesses, and our way of life or "life style." How we see ourselves and others is related to some extent in how we answer these three questions. [1]

With this paragraph Don Hamachek begins his excellent book *Encounter with the Self.* It is no accident that two of our sections are entitled "Who Am I?" and "Where Am I Going?"

In this particular section, we again focus on the student's self-identity and the idea that "I'm glad I'm me!" We also use some of Sid Simon's valuing strategies to begin to get at Hamachek's third question: "Why?"

Don't feel that these exercises are so "heavy" that they might prove threatening to some students. Actually, our experience is that they continue to be fun. The insight that pupils get from doing these activities often comes from the discussion that follows quite naturally. Adults and teenagers especially benefit from talking it over after the exercises.

---

[1] Donald E. Hamachek, *Encounter with the Self* (New York: Holt, Rinehart and Winston, 1971).

ABOUT SCHOOL

Anonymous

This poem was handed to a grade 12 English teacher in Regina, Saskatchewan. Although it is not known if the student actually wrote it himself, it is known that he committed suicide two weeks later.

He always wanted to say things. But no one understood.
He always wanted to explain things. But no one cared.
So he drew.
Sometimes he would just draw and it wasn't anything. He wanted to carve it in stone or write it in the sky.
He would lie out on the grass and look up in the sky and it would be only him and the sky and the things inside that needed saying.
And it was after that, that he drew the picture. It was a beautiful picture. He kept it under the pillow and would let no one see it.
And he would look at it every night and think about it. And when it was dark, and his eyes were closed, he could still see it.
And it was all of him. And he loved it.
When he started school he brought it with him. Not to show anyone, but just to have it with him like a friend.
It was funny about school.
He sat in a square, brown desk like all the other square, brown desks and he thought it should be red.
And his room was a square, brown room. Like all the other rooms. And it was tight and close. And stiff.
He hated to hold the pencil and the chalk, with his arm stiff and his feet flat on the floor, stiff, with the teacher watching and watching.
And then he had to write numbers. And they weren't anything. They were worse than the letters that could be something if you put them together.
And the numbers were tight and square and he hated the whole thing.
The teacher came and spoke to him. She told him to wear a tie like all the other boys. He said he didn't like them and she said it didn't matter.
After that they drew. And he drew all yellow and it was the way he felt about morning. And it was beautiful.
The teacher came and smiled at him. "What's this?" she said. "Why don't you draw something like Ken's drawing?
Isn't that beautiful?"
It was all questions.
After that his mother bought him a tie and he always drew airplanes and rocket ships like everyone else.
And he threw the old picture away.

And when he lay out alone looking at the sky, it was big and blue and all of everything, but he wasn't anymore.

He was square inside and brown, and his hands were stiff, and he was like anyone else. And the thing inside him that needed saying didn't need saying anymore.

It had stopped pushing. It was crushed. Stiff.

Like everything else.

I am smart.
I am capable.
I can do anything that I
   set my mind to do.
It's okay to make mistakes.
I'll just learn from them.
I'm a star.
You're a star.
We are a family and
   we love you.

music and words by miss Victor

Ako

Ako

Kav

r

Hi

A

I

Class Poin

47 owl game

The old owl just sits there and repeats, "Who? Who? Who?" Maybe his "who" is not a question—but then, it might be. In the Owl Game, the "owl" does ask a question, and asks it over and over. He asks his question with sincerity, empathy, and integrity. The respondent must trust his "owl" so he can say whatever pops into his mind. A long philosophical treatise is not an appropriate response; simply a word, phrase, or brief sentence will convey what the respondent is thinking at that moment.

This exercise seems to go better with students of high school age and over.

Ask the students to each find a partner—someone with whom they feel comfortable. Tell them to find a place to sit across from each other and to decide between them who is to be "A" and who is to be "B." After this has been determined, tell the A's that they can only ask the question "Who are you?" The B's, with their eyes closed, are to answer each time with a word or a short phrase. Ask them to continue this until you tell them to stop. Let them go at this in rapid-fire fashion for two to five minutes. Then have them switch roles with B asking "Who are you?" and A answering. Tell the students to say whatever comes into their heads, no matter how crazy, absurd or repetitive it may sound. If they don't, they'll get stuck. Next instruct the A's to ask the question, "Who do you pretend to be?" The B's are to answer as before. Again allow two to five minutes. Then have them switch roles again.

This exercise can be extended or repeated in a variation of this form by using the following questions:

What do you want?	What do you care about?
What do you criticize?	What is your purpose?
What is your next step?	What are you feeling?
What are you crystal clear about?	What do you know?
What do you fear?	Who do you love?

We strongly advise you to allow time for discussion of this activity with the whole class reconvened. Discussion of personal results makes it possible for the students to become aware of both their unique and their common patterns of response. Tuning in to these patterns heightens one's self-awareness.

Adapted from Bernard Gunther, John Hart, and Richard Revheim

48 voting . . . & additional questions

It is necessary to discuss negative or "bad" feelings if one is to develop a healthy self-concept. If a child thinks some of his feelings of hostility, aggression, anger, and hate are unnatural or "bad," he will begin to perceive himself as bad or unnatural. Being able to talk about these feelings in the group has two positive effects on the child's self-image. First, it provides him with an opportunity to defuse some of the feelings by talking them out rather than acting them out in a potentially destructive way. Second, as a child sees that he is not the only one who sometimes wishes his older brother were dead or gets angry with his parents, he will see that his feelings are natural and common responses to similar emotional situations that he shares with his classmates. He will discover that it is acceptable to have these feelings—that it is "O.K." to be the person he is.

To get at negative feelings, let students "vote" by raising their hands to indicate their experience with some of the following types of common childhood problems. Maintain an open and accepting environment of trust and empathy as you ask such questions as:

How many of you:

> Are afraid of ghosts?
>
> Ever get scared?
>
> Like to get angry?
>
> Are afraid when your parents get angry?
>
> Are afraid when your parents fight?
>
> Sometimes want to destroy everything in sight?
>
> Get so mad you could hit someone?
>
> Think you get bossed around too much at home; in school; by your friends; by grown-ups in general?
>
> Like one parent more than the other?

Use your creativity and experience to generate other questions, or ask your students to bring in their own lists of things that evoke negative feelings. Give them the opportunity to discuss any or all of these questions by simply asking, "Would anyone like to say anything about any of the questions?" That is usually all students need to get them into a lively discussion that fosters ventilation and reassurance as they see their feelings are common to others.

You might follow this up by having the children draw a picture of the event that caused the negative feeling to occur, by writing a story about the event, by role-playing or brainstorming alternative procedures for handling such events, and by setting goals to overcome, deal with, or avoid such situations in the future.

We have listed below some samples of other questions to give you an idea of the range of possibilities. Precede each question with a statement such as "How many of you . . ." or "How many here . . ."

Know what you want to do/be when you grow up?

Like to be teased? Sometimes tease others?

Are afraid of the dark? Of wild animals?

Think school is fun? Think school is hard?

Get spanked a lot?

Are the oldest child? The youngest? Middle? Only child?

Cry a lot?

Feel that life could be better for you?

Are in love right now? Wish you were in love right now?

Feel that life has not been fair to you?

Feel happy most of the time?

Feel you have a communication problem with your parents?

Like one of your parents more than the other?

Feel closer to one of your parents than the other?

Get an allowance? Have to work for it?

Would like to change something about the way you look?

Have had a scary dream in the last month?

Think people might not like you if they knew who you really are?

Think people *would* like you if they knew who you really were?

Don't like to talk in class?

Find it easy to make new friends?

Have been in a serious accident?

Have ever wanted to hurt someone for something they did to you?

Would rather be older or younger than you are right now?

Would like to live somewhere else?

Daydream sometimes?

Feel you have to work too hard?

Enjoy being outdoors more than being indoors?

These are just a few ideas to get you started. The best questions come from the concerns and interests of the students themselves. A great idea is to have students make up their own lists of questions and have them or you read it to the class.

Adapted from Sidney B. Simon

49 the ideal model

Many of our behaviors seem to stem from models which we have incorporated sometimes consciously, but more often than not, unconsciously. These models are generally not voluntarily chosen and tend to be derived from social conditioning. They often lack the self-actualizing value of models chosen consciously.

There are two parts to this exercise. The first is designed to help students clarify and articulate the various and conflicting models that determine their behavior at the present time. This prepares the ground for use of the "ideal model" technique in which visualization is used to consciously choose and begin to actualize a model of what we wish to become. Give the following instructions:

A. RECOGNIZING FALSE MODELS

We all have images of ourselves as being less adequate in certain ways than we really are. Consider some of the ways in which you underrate yourself (i.e., putting yourself down, judging yourself, acting as if you are not the kind of person who does this or that easily, etc.). First think about it, writing down ideas that come to you. Then close your eyes and let images or pictures come into your mind which are related to the ways in which you underrate yourself. Study these images for a few minutes, learning as much as you can about them, noting the feelings they arouse in you, and reflecting on their meaning to your life. Write down any insights you have in your journal. (10 to 15 minutes.)

Using the same thought and visualization procedure as above, explore some of the models you have which are based on the way you would like to appear to others (i.e., cool, romantic, carefree, tough guy, good girl, etc.) or the ways you imagine other people would want you to be. There are probably different models involved for the different relationships in your life (e.g., with a boyfriend or girlfriend, with parents, with teachers, with various groups of friends, etc.). Consider these relationships and how you try to appear as contrasted with the way you really are. Become aware of your feelings about each of these roles you play and whether the models they are based on help or hinder your own development. Be specific in trying to articulate and label the models involved. Ask yourself what underlying assumptions you are making in each situation about what behavior is "desirable" in relation to the impression you are trying to create. Remember to use the imaging techniques as well as conscious thought on working on this question. Write down any insights you have in your journal. (10 to 15 minutes.)

B. DISIDENTIFYING FROM THE FALSE MODELS

Imagine and feel what it would be like to let go of all of these false and imposed models of yourself. Realize that they are roles you play or that others would like you to play, but that they do not necessarily define the limits of your existence. You can play these roles if you wish to do so, but you are not locked into them and you can change them if you decide to. Close your eyes and meditate upon the concept of disidentification. (5 minutes.)

C. CHOOSING AN IDEAL MODEL

There are different types of "ideal models," some of a general nature which represent a fully integrated personality, and others of a more specific kind. The most practical type of ideal model to work with in the beginning is one that represents a particular quality or set of interrelated qualities (patience and tolerance or positivity, action and perseverance, serenity) you would like to develop within yourself at this time. These "qualities" can be an underdeveloped psychological function, such as expressing a certain feeling; or an attitude, such as love or calmness; an ability, such as learning to play a musical instrument; or a pattern of action, such as taking a stand for what you believe in. The ideal model must be realistic; it is a vision or a goal to inspire or magnetically "attract" us, but it must represent an attainable next step in our development. If the model feels too idealistic, redefine it until it feels more plausible.

Proceed as you did before, using both rational thought and the imagery technique to choose an ideal model for this point in your development. Take some time to do this. Reflect on what you would like to become and what qualities would help you to accomplish this. See if you can let your thoughts and images come from a place deep within you which is your true essential self. Write down your insights and conclusions. (10 to 15 minutes.)

Please try to follow this activity up with the next one—"The Act as if Technique."

50 act as if

This is a follow-up to the previous "Ideal Model" strategy and should follow it as soon as possible. It is an exercise that works best with high school groups.

People are often encouraged to act "as if" they were great and confident public speakers or mathematicians about to be examined, or highly competent as they go into an interview, or otherwise courageous and confident enough to face a scary situation.

Simple encouragement, however, usually is not enough. A person's "right brain" must be engaged; that is, one must be emotionally involved to function fully in the "as if" mode. This visualization technique will help students practice the use of positive emotion in facing such difficult situations.

After students have chosen an ideal model, they can next be led to visualize themselves in various situations acting *as if* they already possessed the chosen quality, attitude, or ability, to see themselves actually manifesting the *thoughts, feelings, and actions* that correspond to it.

Set up a variety of situations with different people and different circumstances in which students can practice in imagination their new attitudes. They can describe or even act out their visualizations of these new images of themselves carrying out specific new behaviors. They can be directed to notice their own and one another's expressions, postures, gestures, voices, and words as all embodying a new attitude toward the situation.

Suggest that students *feel* what it is like to think and act in this way. If any changes in their ideal models suggest themselves, they should feel free to make whatever corrections or refinements seem desirable. The ideal model is not intended to be static, rigid, and confining. It is flexible, dynamic, and capable of evolving in accordance with one's own development and is the basis of the internal and external feedback received through experience in the world and one's inner promptings.

This can be a very powerful exercise. It is the sort of self-instruction used by peak performers in all walks of life. We usually devote an entire class period to it. It can be followed by a writing assignment or a class discussion.

A young lawyer was sitting at his desk on his first day in his new office. He was eagerly awaiting his first client when he heard the door to his office begin to open. In an attempt to look busy, he picked up the phone and began to talk in a hurried, professional voice.

As he continued his mock conversation, a man entered the office. The young lawyer looked up, motioned for the man to sit down, and then continued his conversation on the phone. Yes, Phil, this Summon s case looks like it is going to be a big one. I thought we ought to bring in Collins from Denver to work with us on it. He s probably the best tax guy in the country, don t you think? Oh, by the way, would you contact Fred over at Solomon and Stone and tell them that we re still willing to discuss a settlement with them, but only if they re willing to come to the table by Friday. Oh, Phil, you re going to have to excuse me, a client just walked in. All right, buddy, talk to you later.

As he hung up the phone, he turned to the man who had just entered the office and said, Yes, sir, how can I help you today?

The man replied, I m here to hook up the phone.

MY PERSONAL STRENGTHS SHEET*

Place a check mark next to each strength that you think you have. You might also have your parents or grandparents go over the list and tell you which ones they think you have, too. Sometimes other people see our strengths more than we do.

- ❏ able to give orders
- ❏ able to take orders
- ❏ able to take care of self
- ❏ accepts advice
- ❏ admires others
- ❏ affectionate
- ❏ alive
- ❏ appreciative
- ❏ articulate
- ❏ artistic
- ❏ assertive
- ❏ athletic
- ❏ attractive

- ❏ bright
- ❏ brave
- ❏ businesslike

- ❏ calm
- ❏ can be firm if necessary
- ❏ caring
- ❏ clean
- ❏ committed
- ❏ common sense
- ❏ communicates well
- ❏ compassionate
- ❏ considerate
- ❏ cooperative
- ❏ courteous
- ❏ creative
- ❏ daring
- ❏ dedicated
- ❏ dependable

- ❏ diligent
- ❏ disciplined
- ❏ do what needs to be done
- ❏ don't give up

- ❏ eager to get along with others
- ❏ eager to please
- ❏ effective
- ❏ efficient
- ❏ elegant
- ❏ encourages others
- ❏ enjoys taking care of others

- ❏ fair
- ❏ feeling
- ❏ forceful
- ❏ frank and honest
- ❏ friendly
- ❏ funny

- ❏ generous
- ❏ gets along with others
- ❏ gets things done
- ❏ gives a lot
- ❏ goal setter
- ❏ good cook
- ❏ good dancer
- ❏ good friend
- ❏ good leader
- ❏ good listener
- ❏ good looking
- ❏ good manners
- ❏ good neighbor
- ❏ good parent

* This page and page 143 can be copied and handed out to your class. They are used in Exercises 38 and 51.

- good singer
- good with details
- good with words
- good with your hands
- graceful
- grateful

- happy
- hard worker
- healthy
- helpful
- honest
- humorous

- independent
- inspiring
- intelligent

- joyful

- keeps agreements
- kind and reassuring

- leadership
- likes responsibility
- lots of friends
- lovable
- loving
- loyal

- makes a difference
- makes a good impression
- mathematical
- mechanical
- motivates others
- musical

- never gives up

- observant
- often admired
- orderly

- organized
- on time
- open

- patient
- peaceful
- physically fit
- pleasant
- positive attitude

- quick learner

- religious
- resilient
- respectful of authority
- respected by others
- responsible
- risk taker

- self-reliant
- self-confident
- self-respecting
- sense of humor
- sensitive
- speaks several languages
- spiritual
- spontaneous
- straightforward and direct
- strong

- team player
- tolerant
- trusting
- truthful

- understanding
- unselfish

- visionary

- warm
- well-dressed

51 adjective wardrobe

Ask the students to tear a piece of paper into eight pieces. On each piece of paper they are to write one word that describes them. Remind them that because no one else will see the slips of paper, they should try to be as honest as possible. Share with your students the "My Strengths Sheets" on pages 142–143 for ideas. When they have completed this, have them arrange the papers in order, placing the one they are most pleased with at the top and the one they are least pleased with at the bottom.

Inform them that what they now have is a wardrobe of descriptive words that they can try on, wear, or discard. Ask them to consider one word at a time. Suggest that they spend a little time considering how they feel about each of the adjectives they have written down. Do they like it? Do they want to keep it? Expand it? Discard it? Or what?

*"The trouble with you, Sheldon, is
you lack self-confidence."*

Ask them to give up each quality one at a time. Do they feel naked? How are they changed? Ask them to fantasize what kind of person they would be with one, two, three, or all of these qualities removed. Have them reclaim the qualities one at a time. How do they feel now?

At the end of the exercise ask each student to record two things he has learned about himself. If there is time, ask the students to share their "I learned . . ." statements. This exercise is somewhat related to "Strength Bombardment" on pages 111–112, which also uses the "My Strengths Sheets."

It was one of the most radical discoveries he [Gandhi] was to make in a lifetime of experimentation: In order to transform others, you have first to transform yourself.

Aknath Easwaran
Gandhi the Man

 **if I were . . .**

This activity is designed to help students clarify who they are, who they want to be, and what they want to do.

Working in groups of three, have the students share what they would be if they were suddenly turned into an animal, a bird, a car, a food, a flower, a musical instrument, or a building. This is usually a very enjoyable exercise, but it is essential that the students try to think of the best representations of their current personality. Ask them to share the reasons for their particular choice with their partners. For example:

> If I were a building, I'd be a small hut on a deserted island. I guess I feel that lonely sometimes.

> If I were a fruit, I'd be a pineapple because pineapples have a hard tough surface, but inside they are soft and sweet.

> If I were a bird, I'd be a canary because I like to sing a lot.

After several minutes of sharing such "If I were's" the class can be encouraged to consider "I would rather be . . ." statements. For example, the student who made the first statement above may add: "But I'd rather be a church so people could find peace in me!" "I would rather be . . ." statements indicate needs or strengths people would like to see actualized in themselves.

A major hang-up affecting educational change is the image we hold of ourselves. Too often we regard ourselves as incapable of effecting change and this apprehension keeps us locked in stereotyped shells incapable of displaying our real humanity. As we understand better the nature of change, we shall likely be unafraid to be genuine, authentic, and real human beings. When this transformation takes place, as it must, we shall then be ready to face the realities involved in change with complete honesty. As real people, we shall learn to prize the learner–his feelings, his opinions, his person. We shall then be able to admit and act upon our admission that it is caring for the learner that counts. Then it is that we shall be able to practice acceptance as the most fundamental law underlying the learning process. Until we are committed to the belief that the other person is a somebody, not a nobody, and that somehow he is trustworthy—until this belief is actualized, we likely will have little interest in effecting worthwhile educational changes.

Dr. A. Craig Phillips

 **if I could be . . .**

This exercise is another way of helping students clarify who they are, what they want to be, and what they want to do. Have the students work in pairs and talk about their written responses to such questions as, "If I could be any animal (bird, insect, flower, food, etc.), I'd be a(n) ___ because . . ." This done, have them form larger groups to share their choices and reasons. Here are some ideas to start with.

If I could be any animal, I'd be a(n) _____ because . . .

If I could be a bird, I'd be a(n) _____ because . . .

If I could be an insect, I'd be a(n) _____ because . . .

If I could be a flower, I'd be a(n) _____ because . . .

If I could be a tree, I'd be a(n) _____ because . . .

If I could be a piece of furniture, I'd be a(n) _____ because . . .

If I could be a musical instrument, I'd be a(n) _____ because . . .

If I could be a building, I'd be a(n) _____ because . . .

If I could be a car, I'd be a(n) _____ because . . .

If I could be a street, I'd be _____ because . . .

If I could be a state, I'd be _____ because . . .

If I could be a foreign country, I'd be _____ because . . .

If I could be a game, I'd be _____ because . . .

If I could be a record, I'd be _____ because . . .

If I could be a TV show, I'd be _____ because . . .

If I could be a movie, I'd be _____ because . . .

If I could be a food, I'd be _____ because . . .

If I could be a part of speech, I'd be a(n) _____ because . . .

If I could be any color, I'd be _____ because . . .

> The teacher as a person is more important than the teacher as a technician. What he is has more effect than anything he does.
>
> Jack Canfield

54 what if . . .

This exercise helps students (and you) become aware of what feelings they have about themselves through the use of projection. It often turns out that even children who do not feel appreciated by people will often project a deeper sense of self-appreciation into the objects discussed in the exercise.

Start the exercise with comments and questions such as:

Did you ever think of things like "What if my bike could talk?" What do you think your bicycle would say about you? Pretend you are something on this list, and tell us what it would say about you.

toothbrush	baseball glove	dresser	radio	brush	doll
bed	school bus	dog	school desk	coat	
shoes	closet	television set	refrigerator	hat	

Have the students verbally share their responses or write their responses as a composition or in their journals. A variation would be to have the students talk about themselves as they imagine their mother, father, brother, sister, teacher, best friend, pet, etc., would talk about them. This variation requires a higher level of trust and openness.

Our experience is that these exercises work best with highly verbal children from about fourth grade up.

Idea by Doris Shallcross

A sense of identity means a sense of being at one with oneself as one grows and develops.

Erik Erikson

---

55 I used to be . . .
but now I'm . . .

Ask the group to sit in a circle. Begin this exercise by saying: I always used to (pause), but now I'm (pause). Can you think of something you used to be or do or think that has changed?

If the statements are incomplete, ask them to make them more complete. For instance, if a student says, "I used to be happy but now I'm not," you should respond, "You used to be happy but now you're not what?"

Examples of student responses have been:

> I used to be worried about someone stealing my bank, but now I'm not worried.

> I used to worry about having awful penmanship, but now I'm working harder.

> I used to be afraid of the dark, but now my mother can shut the door.

> I used to be afraid of the witch at the Halloween party but now I'm not afraid.

An adaptation of this exercise is to have the students write their responses in sentence form on paper. These are handed in and the teacher reads them in random order, thus forming a poem written by the entire class. This can later be typed up and posted or distributed to the students.

For other creative poetry and self-awareness exercises see *Wishes, Lies, and Dreams: Teaching Children to Write Poetry*, by Kenneth Koch (New York: Random House, 1971).

Freedom is the most beautiful, holy and precious fruit of our culture; an individual should never be made to feel that he is at the mercy of any force or coercion or that his will is subjected to others.

Anwar Sadat

---

56 twenty things I like to do

Ask each student to number a sheet of paper from 1 to 20. Then ask them to list twenty things they like to do in whatever order the activities occur to them.

When they have completed this, ask them to annotate each item with the following codes:

Put a dollar sign ($) next to each item that cost over five dollars every time you do it.

Place a P next to each item that you enjoy more when you are doing it with somebody, and an A next to those things you enjoy more when you are doing them alone.

Put a Pl next to each activity that requires planning.

Beside each activity, place the date when you did it last, if you can remember.

Place an F or M next to each item you think your father or mother would have listed when they were your age.

Place an * next to each item you would want your future wife or husband to have on their list. For example:

1. Go surfing   P, Pl, 8/5/92
2. Play basketball   P, Pl, 9/27/92, F
3. Dance   P,   3/38/93, M *
4. Read poetry   3/25/93
5. Go to the movies $, P, Pl, 2/31/93, F

When the students have completed the coding, ask them to make a few "I learned . . ." statements (see Exercise 1). Statements made by students in the past include "I learned I don't need money to be happy." "I learned I like things better when they are spontaneous." "I learned I need to plan more." "I learned I haven't done the things I like to do for a long time."

This would be an opportune time to introduce the concept of goal-setting. Students could be asked to set a goal to do something they like to do, but that they haven't done for a long time (see Exercise 78).

Exercise by Sidney B. Simon

Seek first to understand, then to be understood.

Stephen R. Covey
The Seven Habits of Highly Effective People

	$	P/A	P1	F/M	*	date	You can invent other codes		
1									
2									
3									
4									
5									
6									
7									
8									
9									
10									
11									
12									
13									
14									
15									
16									
17									
18									
19									
20									

I learned that I _____

57 ... the eye of the beholder

This follow-up activity to Exercise 56 is a real reinforcer.

Remind students of the IALAC sign:

I AM LOVABLE AND CAPABLE

In this assertiveness exercise they are to refute in a matter-of-fact way what is said to them or about them. For example,

"My brother says I'm a jerk, but actually I AM LOVABLE AND CAPABLE!"

"My brother sometimes says I'm lazy, but I AM LOVABLE AND CAPABLE!"

After giving these two examples, have your group individually write out things that have been said to them and finish with "but I AM LOVABLE AND CAPABLE!" using capital letters as shown here.

Below is a list of possible sources of putdowns they may have encountered. You might write these on the board as reminders.

My cousin says I'm _____, but I AM LOVABLE AND CAPABLE.

My friend says I'm _____, but

My mother called me _____, but

My neighbor yelled at me for _____, but

My teacher last year said _____, but

My sister says I'm _____, but

My uncle said I'm _____, but

My mother's friend says I'm _____, but

My father says I'm _____, but

The crossing guard said I'm _____, but

A store clerk said I'm _____, but

You or they may think of others. When they've finished, it is fun to share them with their support group or the whole class.

Ann C. Wells

KIDS SEE IT AS _____

Teacher Debbie Monteah of Avondale Middle School in Rochester Hills, Michigan, has her English classes compile two lists: "Kids See It As" first, followed by "Parents See It As".

Some items from her sixth-graders:

A fun toy—a waste of money.

A nightmare vacation—a relaxing trip with the family.

A pair of Reebok pumps—money down the drain.

Your favorite song—a splitting headache.

Try it. You'll like it.

---

58 one of a kind

Start by creating a piece of "art" in front of the class. Don't worry about the quality of the finished product—the uniqueness of the creation is what counts. If you are uncomfortable about this, practice once ahead of time. All you need is a piece of drawing paper, several colors of crepe paper, and a stapler or some paste.

Get the children's attention and then proceed to tear various pieces of crepe paper into jagged free-form patterns, which you then mount on the drawing paper. You may make a "picture," but you'd probably be better off to create a simple design or an abstract expression. It should only take five minutes or less to put together something reasonably attractive and unique. Talk to the class and have fun while you're working (be a ham!). When you've finished your masterpiece, ask:

> *Have you ever seen this before? One exactly like this? What things can you say about this "work of art" that are true? Do you know the meaning of any of these words—"creation," "creative," "create," "creatively?"*

Lead the children to discuss the fact that what you did was create a piece of art. It would be impossible to duplicate the exact creation because the same tears in the paper could not be made, the same paper could not be used, etc. A "picture" that *looks* like yours could be constructed, but it would not be the same work of art.

After you have completed the discussion, ask the children to create their own "masterpieces." Permit them to choose between using crepe paper, construction paper, crayons, or magic markers. Allow about five to ten minutes for this. When the students have completed their creations, ask them to compare them with each other's. Ask if any are the same. They should realize that each work of art is one of a kind.

When they pretty well understand what you're talking about, you should ask:

> Can any of these same ideas we've talked about be applied to human beings?

Again, lead them to a gradual realization through their own thinking that each of them is different, each unique, each irreplaceable and impossible to duplicate.

To be nobody-but-myself—in a world which is doing its best, night and day, to make you everybody else—means to fight the hardest battle which any human being can fight, and never stop fighting.

e. e. cummings
e. e. cummings—a miscellany

 **who's who**

Appoint several students to compile a *Who's Who in the Class*. Data can be gathered such as achievements, hobbies, pets, future aspirations, home addresses, family members, and "favorites"—favorite TV program, favorite food, etc. When the data is collected and written up, see if you can have it duplicated and distributed to all the students.

If facilities are available, pictures can also be used. In addition to publishing a *Who's Who,* you could also have the data posted on a corridor bulletin board to share the information with the rest of the school.

> I've learned that if you pursue happiness, it will elude you. But if you focus on your family, the needs of others, your work, meeting new people, and doing the very best you can, happiness will find you.
>
> a 65-year-old
> *Live and Learn and Pass It On*

60 how do I want to be today?

This is a fine exercise for upper elementary grades through adulthood.

Start by posing the title question on the board in large letters: "How do I want to be today?"

Ask: Have you noticed how some days are much better for you than others? Why do you think that's true? Discuss.

Ask: How does how *you* feel affect your day? Your interactions? Discuss.

Ask: How about your attitude, your intentions—do they affect how your day goes? How? Discuss.

Ask: How about a particular relationship—how do your intentions make it improve or worsen or stay the same? Discuss.

Explain that you're going to ask them to write a kind of Mission Statement. A Mission Statement, in this case, is a brief one-sentence declaration of the goal of their behavior for the immediate future. Some examples:

> "I am going to be friendly and encouraging to everyone I meet."

> "I am going to develop myself as a true student."

> "I am going to control my temper."

The Mission Statement should then be supported with some specific goals. For example, for the first Mission Statement above, the person might write:

1. I am going to thank and hug my mother and tell her I love her.

2. I am going to stop ignoring people I see on the street and, instead, I will smile and say "Hi!"

Now, please read the following to your group:

"HOW I WANT TO BE TODAY" (WRITTEN BY AN ADULT):

I want to experience my spiritual connectedness to all things and all people. (That's his Mission).

1. I'm going to be more considerate to _____ and put her needs first.

2. I'm going to be more compassionate and forgiving of others.

   . . . be a giver, not a taker.

   . . . give the best interpretations of others' behavior: Try to see from their point of view.

3. I'm going to maximize my joy in living, have fun, relax, and not take myself too seriously.

4. I'm going to be less rigid and think "yes" before I think "no."

Have them discuss these ideas by asking the following questions:

What kind of person is the writer?

Do you think he's sincere?

What relationship do you think he was talking about?

Would you like to know him?

Point out that the writer is trying to change himself—not the other person. Is that wise? Why? When your group is ready, ask them to write their own genuine statement entitled "How Do I Want to Be Today," starting with a Mission Statement, which will then be supported by some specific goals. (You may want to put a rudimentary outline on the board.)

When they're satisfied with what they have written, have them rewrite their statements onto 5" × 7" cards, which they can keep as handy reminders for as long as they wish.

The person who wrote the example above has referred to it periodically for at least two years and has been refreshed in his efforts to change each time he reads it.

This activity can be extended and strengthened by using visualizations and affirmations. In the quiet of her room each morning and evening, a student can visualize herself being the kind of person she wants to be, including expressing the qualities she wants to manifest and the achievement of her goals. Affirmations again support and strengthen efforts. The man in the example above might compose an affirmation like: "I am happily experiencing my connectedness to all living things."

DRAW ME CAPABLE!

COLOR ME HAPPY!

CALL ME SPECIAL!

Harold Clive Wells

61 public interview

This method of enhancing self-esteem has great possibilities, but it should be used with caution; the classroom climate should be friendly, warm, and accepting before it is used.

The purpose of the public interview is to gain a deeper knowledge of the student, to give the student the opportunity to publicly receive the attention of all his classmates, to suggest life alternatives to others, and to show students that they are not alone in many of their feelings.

Ask for a volunteer to be interviewed in public. Then ask the selected student to stand in front of the class. Ask a series of questions (appropriate to the age level). The student may choose to answer the questions or to "pass." It is important that the right to pass is made explicit.

The interview may be terminated at any time by either of the participants, especially the student being interviewed. A simple statement like "Thank you for the questions" automatically brings the interview to a stop.

At the end of the interview, the student may ask the interviewer any of the same questions that were asked him. Interview information may be recorded and used as a page for the student's journal.

Some sample interview questions are:

1. What is your favorite sport?
2. What do you like best about school? Least about school?
3. What kind of TV programs do you like to watch?
4. What would you do with $1,000? With $1,000,000?
5. If you were a teacher, how would you teach your class?
6. Do you have a hobby that takes up a lot of your time? What is it? How did you get interested in it?
7. What is your idea of a perfect Saturday afternoon?
8. What changes would you make to improve the school?
9. Have you ever invented anything? What?
10. What is the best news you could get now?
11. Is there something you want badly but can't afford right now?

12. Do you work after school or on the weekends? Where? What are you using the money for?

13. If you had three wishes, what would they be?

14. What is the best thing that ever happened to you?

15. Can you think of something you would be willing to say to the class that you think might be good for them to hear?

16. If you had a chance to go on a spaceship, would you go? Why or why not?

17. Have you ever moved to a different house or apartment? How did you feel about that? Why?

SECRET PLACE

I run down to my secret place
a creek
I lie down
on the
    new
      soft
        cool
          green
            grass
and
    fall
      asleep
        to
          the
            sound of the gurgling creek
and the
    sweet
      song
        of
        a
        sparrow
        in a nearby tree.
        I fall into another world
        of curiosity and
dreams.

by Autumn Chalker
Mrs. Bynum's fifth-grade class
Buckley, Michigan, Community School

62 the public statement

Whenever it is requested, allow students a short period of time, say five minutes, to make a public statement to the class. This could be done any time there is an extra five minutes available. The student's statement should be about something that he wants to say to his classmates. It may be a statement of criticism or of public affirmation. It may be highly emotional or extremely objective. In any case, it comes solely from the student and is not to be censored or countered by the teacher or the rest of the class. It is to be a public statement without rebuttal. Other students may wish to react at a later date with statements of their own addressed to the same topic, but a debate should not be allowed to develop.

If a person's self-concept is to grow, he must have the opportunity to publicly affirm the things he believes in. This experience also provides the student with temporary control over his environment, for during the public statement he has control of all the ears in the room; those precious few moments are his and his alone. The public statement also indicates to the class that the teacher respects student ideas.

As an alternative, ask the students to submit opinion papers on whatever they would care to voice an opinion about. Opinion papers might be submitted as a reaction to someone else's public statement. These papers should not be corrected or graded.

A circus owner bought a most remarkable crow. Next night, his wife told him that she had cooked it. "Cooked it!" howled the owner. "Good grief, that bird could speak eight languages!" "So," shrugged the wife, "why didn't it say something?"

63 motorcycle fantasy

In several places in this book, we've used different guided visualizations to help a student get some insight into his personality. This is another such exercise. It has special appeal to youth because motorcycling is so popular with them.

Prepare your class for a brief guided visualization experience. The children should be relaxed, happy, sitting with their eyes closed. Speak softly but clearly and pause briefly between sentences so they have time to visualize an answer to your directions and questions.

> *Imagine that you are a motorcycle. Notice what kind you are and what make and model. Notice where you are kept when you are not being ridden. How do you feel about it? Are you maintained well? Imagine you are being started. Do you start easy or hard? What kind of noise do you make? You are being ridden now. Notice who your rider is. How do you get along with each other? Have a dialogue with your rider; finish the dialogue and become aware of how fast you are going. Notice where you are. What kind of condition are you, the motorcycle, in? Notice all of your various parts. Is everything working smoothly? Any badly worn parts about to cause trouble? Where are you now? What kind of road are you driving on? Is there a lot of traffic or just a little? Notice how you feel being a motorcycle. Your left handlebar has a brake grip for the front wheel, and your right handlebar has the acceleration grip. Carry on a dialogue or coversation between the front wheel brake grip on the left and the accelerator on the right. Notice carefully what each is saying and feeling. You are being stopped now. Where did you stop and how? How do you feel after your ride?*

Ask the students to take a few moments to write and/or draw what they got in touch with. Ask them to note any parallels to their own life. For example, if they were left out in the rain and not maintained well, maybe they feel uncared for in their own lives.

Afterwards, break the students into groups of three or four to discuss their experiences. When discussing the motorcycle, ask them to speak in the first person: "I am a large, powerful Harley Davidson. I make a lot of noise, and everywhere I go people notice me." This visualization usually leads to an animated discussion. Don't interpret or suggest "good" and "bad" concerning any student's content. Let your students take what they can from the activity without pressing for too much insight.

This visualization was suggested by John O. Stevens.

Anything you can do to increase communication in your class will reduce your need to impose order by authority, and reduce the student's need to rebel against that authority. The class will become more a place for listening and learning, and less a place for fighting and antagonism.

John O. Stevens
Awareness

accepting my body

According to recent research, only 4% of American adults like their body the way it is now! This disapproval of our physical selves starts early and doesn't seem to leave us until old age—if then.

The connection between our physical selves and own self-concept/self-esteem is obvious. What we've done in this section—a considerable improvement over the first edition—is to try to get students to look at their bodies in a more positive light.

One way of doing this is to take perceived weaknesses and mentally transform them into assets. Another is to treat this whole body image problem with a greater degree of acceptance. We want students to have the attitude that "If you can't change it, smile, accept it, and forge ahead."

This is not to say that kids can just laugh off their appearance. Of course, they can't—or won't—and we, too, take it seriously. But, then, a smile is ever helpful on the face of any of us!

Another aspect of this body image problem is the isolation we feel when we're not physically touched. This rewritten section gives more attention to the benefits of being affectionately "in contact" with one another.

165

64 oh nose, I love you!

This activity has been lots of fun for students, teachers, counselors, and group leaders.

It deals with body image by asking people to identify some part of their body they *don't* like and then transform that into a positive characteristic.

Start by asking students to identify, either out loud or on paper, a part of their body they don't like. (Actress Meryl Streep, of all people, identified her nose.)

Ask them to write a paean (hymn of praise) to that part of their body—for example:

> *Ah, this lovely nose of mine is the source of such great joy because it senses out those delicious odors of bread baking, popcorn popping, and roses blooming, not to mention bacon and eggs frying over a hardwood campfire! Oh, what ecstasy; what a bright and shining beacon my nose is—cutting through the air as I whiz downhill on my bike. Dear nose, I love you!*

It might be of interest to junior high or middle school students to read the wonderful language of Rostand in *Cyrano de Bergerac* as Cyrano describes his own very large nose in exaggerated terms. Ask your students to collect other examples from literature.

You get the idea. Have students share the delightful expositions in a small group or with the whole class.

Harold Clive Wells and Ann C. Wells

I think, therefore I am. ⟶

⟵ Descartes

I feel, therefore I am. ⟶

⟵ Thomas Jefferson

I smell, therefore I am.

⟵ The Nose of Harold Clive Wells

My nose, sir, is enormous. Cretinous moron! A man ought to be proud of such an appendage!

A great nose may be an index of a great soul, kind, endowed with liberty and courage—like mine!

Edmund Rostand
Cyrano de Bergerac

65 some body games

RAG DOLL—TIN SOLDIER

This exercise loosens people up by having them make contact with each other in a playful way. Ask the students to choose partners of approximately the same physical size. When they are in pairs, ask them to designate themselves A and B. Tell them that in the first round A's will be tin soldiers and B's will be their directors. Tin soldiers can only move forward. They have no power to think or make decisions. Demonstrate for the students how a tin soldier walks: slowly, with stiff legs and arm joints—like a toy tin soldier. Then tell them that B's job is to guide his tin soldier and to turn him so as to avoid hitting walls, tables, and other tin soldiers walking around the room. Now have the B's wind up their tin soldiers and turn them on. Things often get quite rambunctious in this exercise, but as long as things don't get too chaotic, let it happen. The students enjoy it!

After a few minutes, stop the action and have them reverse roles so that B is now the tin soldier with A leading. Again after a few minutes, stop them and give them these new instructions.

A's are to be on their backs on the floor. They are to become totally limp, like rag dolls. B's job is to stand them up. It is an almost impossible task if the A's remain limp. The exercise is a lot of fun. Again after a few minutes, reverse roles.

After all segments of the exercise have been completed, bring the students together in a circle and ask them to share what that was like for them. Ask questions such as: How did you feel? Was it fun? What did you do? What were you thinking about when you were the leader? Was it easier to be the tin soldier or the leader? Was it frustrating trying to stand your rag doll up? As you get into this, you'll find that more questions will come to mind. If nobody has much of anything to say, that's O.K., too. Remember this is just a warm up, so simply go on to another exercise.

FREEZE TAG

This exercise works best in a large open space with a big group. Arbitrarily designate about one-fourth to one-third of the group as "it." This can be done by designating all those wearing the color red, or tennis shoes, or those over ten years of age, or whatever. These are the "freezers." Their task is to freeze the rest of the group. They do this by tagging someone and yelling "Freeze!" The person tagged must stop and freeze in his position at the time he is tagged. Although this sounds simple, the catch is that anyone still unfrozen may unfreeze a frozen member by touching him and yelling "Unfreeze." The game is a lot of fun and generates a lot of energy. It is good for a sleepy group and can be played with as many as 100 people in a gymnasium.

THE HUMAN PRETZEL

Ask for someone in the class who likes to solve puzzles. Send that person out of the room or into a corner with his eyes closed for a minute. The rest of the class joins hands in a circle. Then, without breaking the hand contact, they tangle themselves up by going under, over, in, and out of each other's arms. When the class is thoroughly entangled, ask the detective to return and try to untangle the group by giving verbal instructions to different people as to how they should move.

STATUES

Ask the students to choose partners, and have them designate themselves A and B. A's are to be sculptors and B's are to be clay. A's job is to mold B into a statue that expresses how he (A) is feeling right now. When this is done (allow a few minutes), ask the B's to tell the A's how they imagine they must be feeling. Give them a few minutes for sharing and then reverse the process.

MIRRORING

Have the class stand in two evenly matched rows, both facing the same direction (with one student standing in back of another student). Have the students in the front row begin to move their whole bodies, including their arms and their legs. Have the students in the back row try to exactly copy every move of the student directly in front of him. Allow about three to four minutes for this.

Now have all the children turn and face the opposite direction. Repeat as above, having the students in the front row move and the students in the back row copy. Again allow about three minutes for this.

Explain to the students that this is called "mirroring." Take a few minutes to talk about a real mirror and what happens when we look into one.

Now have the students face each other. Have one be the "mirror," the one who copies exactly, and the other the "doer," the one who controls the mirror's actions. Allow about three minutes for this. Then change roles and allow another three minutes. Encourage the students to use their whole body, including facial expressions. Suggest that they can try to turn around together, make funny faces, jump up and down, etc.

After the exercise is over, ask the students to talk about which role was easier for them—leading or following. With older students, you can ask them to think about what the world would be like if everyone always wanted to lead and there were no followers, or vice versa. How might their individual preference for leading or following affect their behavior in the class? What is difficult about leading (being judged, feeling the pressure to be creative or funny, feeling awkward, etc.) and about following (giving up control to another person, feeling inferior, not doing it well, being asked to do some movement that isn't comfortable, etc.)? What are the advantages of leading and of following? How do they feel when they are dancing and they are the leader or the follower? Do they make up steps or imitate others?

We learned this version of the mirroring exercise from Gloria Castillo.

66 student photographs

Many students will have photographs of themselves from home, school, dime-store booths, etc. If enough students have these pictures, they can be mounted on different-colored construction paper and placed on a bulletin board with interesting biographical material included.

If pictures are not readily available, you may want to take pictures of the students with a automatic 35mm camera. Such cameras are available at reasonable cost or can be borrowed.

A variation of this activity is to compare students' baby pictures with their current photos. If enough baby pictures are available, it is fun to have the class try to guess the identity of the person in each picture. This variation reinforces the fact that everyone has distinct features and unique characteristics, as well as illustrates the concept of change and growth.

> A friend of mine traveling in Mexico saw a beautiful child and asked permission of the mother to photograph him. She was pleased by the request but when the photographer was leaving she stopped him and said, "Touch him," and then she added, "A child that is not touched will be unlucky."
>
> Laura Huxley
> *You Are Not the Target*

67 fingerprints

The purpose of this activity is to demonstrate that everyone is unique and different in many ways—one of which is their fingerprints.

Have the children divide themselves into groups of five, and supply each group with an ink pad. After cautioning them about getting ink on their clothing, ask them to make their fingerprints by first pressing their fingers on an ink pad and then on a sheet of white paper. The best print is obtained by rolling the finger from left to right without squeezing down too hard. Using magnifying glasses, have them carefully study and compare each others' prints.

After they have done this, ask the children if they have any ideas of how policemen use fingerprints to catch criminals. Everyone's fingerprints are unique and different. They can used to identify one another.

Some other ways authorities use to identify people are with voice prints, footprints, and dentition. In each of these cases, as in others, there is sufficient uniqueness to identify an individual.

This is a good place to note that students also have different learning styles. These learning styles apply to how they process information, how they prefer to study, and how they relate to others.

Every person needs recognition. It is expressed cogently by the lad who says, "Mother, let's play darts. I'll throw the darts and you say 'Wonderful.'"

M. Dale Baughman
Educator's Handbook of Stories, Quotes, and Humor

68 · the affectionate laying on of hands

Many years ago, at McKinley Elementary School in Livonia, Michigan, the staff engaged in a concerted year-long effort to raise children's self-esteem. Every weekly faculty meeting was devoted, in part, to sharing the teachers' knowledge, readings, and efforts. Second-grade teacher Walt Schumacher decided to try what he whimsically called "the affectionate laying on of hands."

Walt's idea was to touch each child each day as a way of recognizing and affirming that student. Usually it meant putting his hand on a pupil's forearm or shoulder as he talked with him or her.

Years later, we read that Marine Corps recruiters had found a remarkable success ratio in getting qualified young men to join the Marines by the simple expedient of touching the potential recruit at some time during the recruitment presentation! Imagine that! If it's good enough for the Marines, it's good enough for us!

There are, in fact, few things as sweet to human beings as the warm, affectionate touch of another person.

Someone has said that emotional CPR consists of "one hug, one deep breath. Repeat!"

Touch is vital to life. Virginia Satir wrote that the recommended daily requirement for hugs is: four per day for survival, eight per day for maintenance, and twelve per day for growth. We need to be caressed, cuddled, and stroked as much as we need food. Babies who are deprived of touch can actually die: lacking stimulation and nurturance, their spines shrivel up.

A scientist from the National Institutes of Health claims that lack of touch and pleasure during the formative years of life is the principal cause of human violence. He claims that individuals and societies that experience and promote physical pleasure are also peaceful societies. "As either violence or pleasure goes up, the other goes down," states J. W. Prescott.

Louise Hart
The Winning Family

69 the trust walk

This exercise is best done after students have gotten to know each other fairly well. It greatly adds to the level of trust and closeness in a class.

Ask the students to pick a partner they feel friendly with or close to. (After the initial exposure to this exercise, you can have them pick partners with people they feel that they don't know very well.) Tell them that they will be going on a walk together in which one person will have his eyes closed and the other will be guiding him. Ask them to decide who would like to be the first with their eyes closed. When they have decided, tell them that the guide's job is to make sure that their partner is safe at all times—i.e., doesn't bump into anything or fall down the stairs. The guides should also try to give their partner as interesting a walk as possible. They can take their partners up and down stairs, into places that have different noises, walk them backwards, run and jump with them, go in circles, etc. They can also give their partner a variety of different sensory experiences by placing their hands on objects with different textures such as smooth glass, rough concrete, a soft carpet, a water fountain, a pile of towels, a fur coat, the keys of a piano, etc. Ask them to use their ingenuity and imagination.

Tell them that this entire exercise is to be done without talking. Both partners are to be silent the whole time. After about ten or fifteen minutes, using a prearranged signal (a bell, a record player, a trumpet blast, etc.), have them switch roles. After another ten to fifteen minutes, have them return to the group and share their experiences. You can facilitate the discussion with such questions as:

Were you able to trust your partner with your eyes closed?

Did you open your eyes at any time?

Did you find it easier following or leading? What was easy or hard about it?

Did you enjoy the exercise? What did you enjoy about it?

Trust is the result of a risk successfully survived.

Jack R. Gibb

70 body tracing

Ask the students to form pairs. Have each student lie down on a piece of heavy brown wrapping paper while his partner traces an outline of his body. The students can then cut the figures out and color them.

This provides a life-sized self-portrait for each child. When the pictures are completed, the teacher can put them up around the room for display.

You may wish to keep the pictures, repeat the exercise at the end of the year, and have the class compare their new figures with their earlier productions.

To add to the impact of this exercise, ask each child to write a short story describing himself entitled "This Is Me." Tape these stories onto the hands of the students' self-portraits.

A good variation for high school students is to have them trace an outline of their body and then to create a giant collage by filling in the body with pictures and words cut out of magazines and newspapers. Prepare for this exercise by having the students bring copies of magazines and other sources of pictures to class. You may wish to talk with a local newsstand about getting free copies of remainders—magazines that have not sold.

Have the students share their creations in small groups or with the whole class.

> Each human being is born as something new, something that never existed before. He is born with what he needs to win at life. Each person in his own way can see, hear, touch, taste, and think for himself. Each has his own unique potentials—his capabilities and limitations. Each can be a significant, thinking, aware, and creatively productive person in his own right—a winner.
>
> Muriel James and Dorothy Jongeward
> *Born to Win: Transactional Analysis with Gestalt Experiments*

71 seven for the road

1. What is your body part (e.g., neck, arm, hand) saying to you today? If it is negative, rewrite it to say something nice about it and you.

2. List ten things your body can do that are pleasing to you.

3. Write a short poem entitled: "My Body!"

4. Have mirrors in the class where children can observe themselves. You can also have them carry on dialogues with themselves in the mirror, describe what they see, make funny faces, check for smiles before an activity, or engage in "through the looking-glass" fantasies about how they would appear if larger, smaller, elongated, or compressed.

5. Write a brief essay entitled: "How I Can Make the Most of My Looks."

6. Have your group take a smile or laughter break.

7. Have your students write "A Letter from the Interior." Ask them to pretend that their body could write them a letter. What would it say? It might include things like "I need more sleep. Why don't you ever exercise me? I feel undervalued and underappreciated. And by the way, what do you expect me to do with the junk you put into my stomach? When I am full of pizza and ice cream and potato chips, I can't digest it all properly. It's like a big mess of play dough down here. Give me a break!"

72 I love myself

People are reluctant to say, "I love myself," because they've been so indoctrinated in the idea that one must be humble and that pride can be ugly, even sinful. Humans are more apt to say "like" than "love," when referring to themselves. Nevertheless, we feel that students ought to be encouraged to love themselves and be able to say it without false modesty or its opposite, silly or neurotic bravado.

What we know about human psychology is that acceptance *by* ourselves *of* ourselves as we are, with all of our failings, warts, occasional stupid behaviors, and faults, is the first step toward good mental health.

This exercise is fun and should be conducted when you and the students are in a relaxed and happy mood. We've found the best approach is to dictate to the class slowly, pausing to give students time to fill in the blanks. This requires each one to write out complete self-affirming sentences, which, in turn, reinforce the positive messages. This exercise is appropriate for middle school age students up to adults.

Have the class poised and ready to take dictation under the heading "I Love Myself." Students should write the whole sentence or sentences in completed form.

I love myself because . . .

I love myself even though . . .

Yes, I love myself even though I sometimes . . .

It's not so bad to . . .

I forgive myself for . . .

I can change some things about myself that I'm not crazy about. For example, I can change . . .

I will change that! I'm going to start now by . . .

Instead, I can . . .

Even though I can't change . . . I love myself. I can live with that because doing this makes me feel good about myself.

I am in control of my life.

I have power.

I really like who I am.

I am very optimistic about the future.

Oh, yes, I love myself because . . .

I totally and unconditionally love myself just the way I am.

I am always growing and changing. I am becoming better every day.

You may want the students to share what they have written in small groups of two to four people or with the whole class. Sharing in a trusting environment builds confidence and self-esteem. It gives others a chance to see themselves more clearly as they reflect on their own and their classmates' self-disclosures.

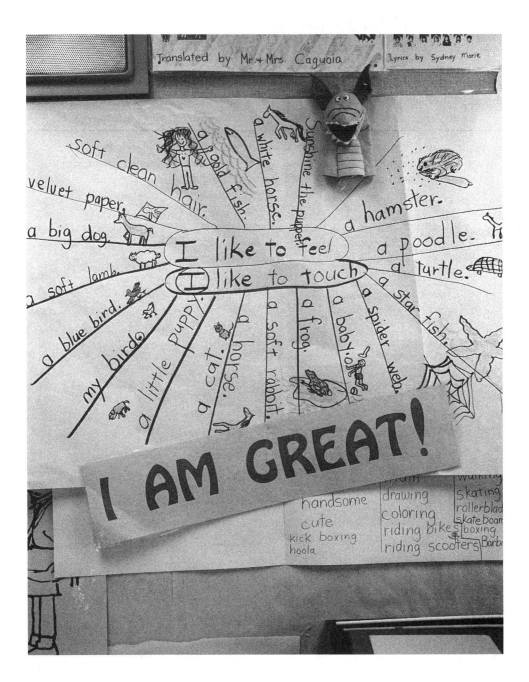

73 sensory awareness

> We conclude, then, that the study of mammal, monkey, ape, and human behavior clearly shows that touch is a basic behavioral need, much as breathing is a basic physical need, that the dependent infant is designed to grow and develop socially through contact, tactile behavior, and throughout life to maintain contact with others. Furthermore, that when the need for touch remains unsatisfied, abnormal behavior will result.
>
> Ashley Montague
> *Touching*

Owing to a lack of regard for sensory development, the people we teach are often out of touch with themselves and each other. As we teach children to "keep their hands to themselves," we soon find that they are out of contact with one another.

We have collected a series of sensory awareness exercises that you can use in your classroom. As you do them, take your time—don't rush through them. When people have completed one or several exercises, allow them an opportunity to discuss what they have experienced.

1. Close your eyes and become aware of how your head feels. Bend your fingers at the joints and tap all over the top of your head. Tap the back, the sides, and the forehead. Put your hands down and experience how your head and hands feel.

2. Close your eyes and experience how your face feels. Keeping your eyes closed, begin slapping your forehead with your fingers. Both hands and fingers should be held loosely and hit the face simultaneously. Now move to the jaw, the cheeks, the lips, and the chin. Go over the nose and gently over the eyelids. Stop, lower your hands, and experience what you feel now. This slapping can be done on any or all sections of the body. You can do it yourself or with a partner.

3. Pick a partner the same sex as you. Mentally divide his body in half—right side and left side. Concentrating only on the left side, tap all over your partner's head, and then slap his shoulders and left arm, back, stomach, left leg, and foot. The person being tapped keeps his eyes closed. When this is completed, both you and your partner should stand with eyes closed and experience your own bodies. After a minute or two you should share

how you experience the difference between your right and left sides. After you have reported, the procedure should be repeated on the right side so you will feel balanced again.

4. For the entire class period, use your left hand (if left-handed, use your right). Do everything you can with your weaker side. Become aware of how you feel doing this. What do you experience? Are you able to be patient with yourself? How do you experience yourself at the end of the class?

5. Pick a partner. Sit facing him. Take both of your partner's hands in both of yours. Close your eyes. Feel the contact where your hands stop and his start. Keeping your eyes closed and without *verbal* interaction, have a conversation with your hands. Allow yourself to be shy at first, then be bold. Test your partner's strength and express yours. Now have an argument. Make up. Be gentle with each other. Now express your playfulness. Now create a dance together. Let the dance subside. Say goodbye. Withdraw contact. Experience how you feel now. Open your eyes and look at your partner. Now discuss your experience with him.

6. Inhale through your nose for the count of eight. As you breathe in, let your stomach come out. Then exhale through your mouth for the count of eight, letting your stomach come in. Repeat this fifteen times. This is a good exercise at the beginning of a class when all the students' energies seem to be scattered. We have also found it useful as a way to relax students before they take a test.

7. Everyone stand or sit in a circle, all facing one direction so that you are each directly behind another person. Reach out to the person in front of you and massage her neck and shoulders (3 minutes). Now turn around and do the same thing to the person who is behind you (3 minutes). This way, everyone is both simultaneously giving and receiving a massage.

8. The entire class starts to walk around. Shake both hands of each person you meet. Then shake the elbows of each person you meet. Now shake each others' shoulders. Continue on with legs, heads, and noses. Afterward, stop, close your eyes, and become aware of how you feel.

> Education ideally is an active, interested exploration: skill, learning, knowing, doing. Too much of formal education is dulling, memorization, passive compartmentalization, indoctrination.
>
> Bernard Gunther
> *Sense Relaxation*

74 weather report

This exercise is an adaptation of work some New Zealand nurses do in teaching potentially abusing mothers how to touch their children in healthy, loving ways. We saw this described in Dr. Louise Hart's *The Winning Family*. It seems to us that teachers can usefully adapt this for occasional use with particularly needy youngsters.

The teacher is the provider of the touch. The student is the receiver, is in charge, and should give feedback. The touching is given in the following sequence, with the teacher pleasantly announcing the advent of each new weather condition.

Snowflakes	Tap your fingertips rapidly and very lightly on the head, shoulders and back.
Raindrops	Tap your fingertips simultaneously with somewhat greater intensity.
Thunderclaps	With cupped palms, clap hands across the child's back, but not too hard.
Tidal wave	Slide your hands in long strokes up and down the student's arms and across the back.
Calm	Rest your hands on his shoulder for a few moments. Hold them one-half inch above his back for a few moments, then step back.

Nonverbal reassurance and physical contact also are vital to a healthy childhood. Nonverbal communication can be as simple as an encouraging smile and as reassuring as a firm hug.

Children's Television Workshop
Raising Responsible Kids

75 why I like myself

Ask *primary* children to name the different people they like. They will probably name their parents, friends, grandparents, neighbors, or special relatives. If they don't name themselves, ask: "What about yourself? Do you like you?" Impress on them that it is very important to like yourself. When they do say they like themselves, carry this idea out by saying, "Think about yourself. What do you like about: (1) how you look? (2) how you play? (3) how you act? (4) what you do." (Talk about each category for a few minutes.)

Fold 9" × 12" construction paper in half, lengthwise. Rip along folded crease. Put two sections together, fold crosswise, and staple to make a booklet. You could use more paper to make a thicker book if desired.

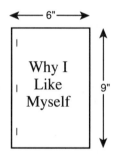

Have the children make a *Why I Like Myself* booklet by drawing pictures to show what they like about themselves. Ask children to share these with their friends and talk about them.

THE CYCLE OF SUCCESS

COMPLETE THE PAST
• The mirror exercise
• Acknowledge successes

CELEBRATE
YOUR SUCCESS
• Reward yourself
• Thank others

POSITIVE SELF-TALK
• "I Can" attitude
• Accept responsibility

1

10

2

PERSEVERE
• Never give up
• Fallure is just a step
toward success

IDENTIFY YOUR STRENGHTS
• Do regular inventories
• Ask people you trust

9

3

The Cycle
of Success

RESPOND TO
FEEDBACK
• Solicit feedback
• Take corrective
action

8

4

CLARIFY YOUR PURPOSE
AND YOUR VISION
• A mission that motivates
• Share it

7

5

ACT TO CREATE IT
• Take action
• Ask, ask, ask
• Do it now!

6

SET GOALS AND OBJECTIVES
• Be specific
• Write them down

VISUALIZE AND
AFFIRM YOUR SUCCESS
• Write your own affirmations
• Visualize them as accomplished

190

where am I going?

After studying successful people in all walks of life, we discovered that most of them have practiced ten specific steps to success. We also learned that these steps and the skills associated with them are teachable to any age student. Some of these skills have been introduced already and others are incorporated in this and later sections.

This repetition is deliberate on our part because we feel that these principles and skills need to be taught and retaught many times; for example, the strategies of visualization and affirmations are suggested in several of the activities throughout the book.

THE 10 STEPS TO SUCCESS

1. Acknowledge the Positive Past:

- Let go of your past hurts. (Feel it . . . Forgive . . . and Forget)
- Do the mirror exercises every morning and night.
- Keep a "Victory Log"—Write down all of your successes everyday.

2. Positive Self-Talk:

- Use only positive self-talk ("I can . . ." and "I will . . .")
- Do not use "I can't . . .", "I'll never," or, "They made me . . ."
- If you think a negative thought, whack the vulture!
- If someone puts you down, say

"NO MATTER WHAT YOU SAY OR DO TO ME,
I'M STILL A WORTHWHILE PERSON."

3. Acknowledge and Affirm Your Strengths:

- Write down all of your personal strengths.
- Ask others to tell you what they see as your strengths.
- Review the "My Strengths," sheet every week.

4. Clarify Your Vision and Your Values:

- Decide what is important to you.
- Notice whom you admire and what you admire about them; then create a plan to become more like them.

5. Plan Your Future:

- Set goals.
- Write your goals down . . . make them specific and measurable.

6. Visualize and Affirm Your Success:

- Say your affirmations. Close your eyes and see yourself as a winner. Do this every day when you wake up, at lunch time, and before you go to bed.

7. Act to Create It:

- TAKE ACTION . . . DO IT NOW.
- Act as if you have already reached your goal.
- ASK, ASK, ASK, ASK, ASK for what you need and want UNTIL YOU GET IT!

8. Respond to Feedback:

- Look for feedback and ask for feedback.
- When you are "off course," get back "on course."
- Remember: It's O.K. to make mistakes. Just learn from them.

9. Persevere:

- Never give up your dream.
- Keep on keepin' on.

- Remember: There is no such thing as failure. Failure means a second chance to reach your goal.

10. Reap the Rewards:

   - When you reach your goal, give yourself a reward.
   - Thank other people who have helped you reach your goal.

 **twenty-one questions**

Hand out a sheet to each of your students with the following questions on it. Ask them to write the answers to any or all questions in whatever order they wish. When they have finished, have them discuss their answers in small groups, make "I learned . . ." statements, or discuss how the assignment made them feel. The students may want to record their responses in their journals.

1. What would you like to do, have, accomplish?
2. What do you wish would happen?
3. What would you like to do better?
4. What do you wish you had more time for? More money for?
5. What more would you like to get out of life?
6. What are your unfulfilled ambitions?
7. What angered you recently?
8. What made you tense, anxious?
9. What have you complained about?
10. What misunderstandings did you have?
11. With whom would you like to get along better?
12. What changes for the worse or better do you sense in the attitudes of others?
13. What would you like to get others to do?
14. What changes will you have to introduce?
15. What takes too long?
16. What are you wasting?
17. What is too complicated?
18. What "bottlenecks" or blocks exist in your life?
19. In what ways are you inefficient?
20. What wears you out?
21. What would you like to organize better?

This is also a good time to introduce goal-setting to your students as a technique for gaining control over their lives and achieving at least one of the things mentioned above.

Suggested by Doris Shallcross

First say to yourself what you would be; and then do what you have to do.
Epictetus
Discourses

77 four drawings

Supply each student with a box of crayons and a large sheet of newsprint (if not available, use four sheets of 8½ × 11 inch paper instead). Ask the students to divide the paper into four equal sections. Tell them that they are going to draw four pictures depicting the symbolic answers to four questions you are going to have them ask themselves.

Ask them to close their eyes. You may also wish to help them to become more relaxed by doing a deep-breathing exercise or by simply taking a minute to stretch out any tensions they may feel in their bodies. After they have had a minute or two to relax their bodies, ask them to let go of any emotions they may be feeling at the moment. Finally, ask them to quiet all the chatter of their minds so that they can become receptive to messages from their intuitive self, their true center. Tell them to imagine a blank movie screen in the middle of their forehead just above their nose. Tell them that you are going to give them a question to ask themselves, and that they should let an image be projected onto their movie screen that will represent or symbolize the answer. As soon as they have seen the image (no matter what the image is, or how unrelated it may at first seem), they are to draw it in the upper left-hand section of their papers. The later drawings will go in the remaining sections. Have them number each picture in order.

The four questions are:

1. Where am I?
2. Where am I going?
3. What obstacles will I face?
4. What inner quality will I need to develop to overcome these obstacles?

Allow about eight to ten minutes for each question and drawing. After they have completed all four drawings, ask them to share them in groups of three or four.

As you might have guessed, this exercise works best with high school age and older.

We learned this exercise from Martha Crampton and George Brown.

Perhaps the most important single cause of a person's success or failure educationally has to do with the question of what he believes about himself.
Arthur W. Combs
Perceiving, Behaving, and Becoming

78 the goalpost

Decorate the bulletin board in the form of a football goalpost. Each day allow time for the students who would like to set a goal for that day or week to record them on 3 × 5 inch index cards and post them on the bulletin board below the crossbar of the goalpost. If time permits, you may wish to have the class cut the index cards into the shape of footballs.

On the following day, ask all those who completed their goals to move their index cards above the crossbar and to share their goal and how they completed it with the class. This provides the goal-achievers with the attention of their peer group as a reinforcement to their action.

Those who did not complete their goals are not allowed to share with the class their goals and the reasons for not accomplishing them. (If they did this, they would be receiving the same reinforcement of peer attention as those who had completed theirs. The class would also be reinforcing their behavior of rationalizing away their failure to take responsibility for achieving their goals.)

This is a powerfully important exercise in that it makes explicit accomplishments that are often overlooked. It also helps students to focus on the development of the will. Another positive by-product is often improved home relationships. For example, one third-grade girl began to set goals like clearing the table without being asked, helping to do the dishes, taking out the garbage, cleaning her room, etc. A week later her amazed mother called her teacher and wanted to know what had happened.

We have found the guidelines on the next page very helpful for effective goal-setting.

"Cheshire-Puss," she began, rather timidly . . . "Would you tell me, please, which way I ought to go from here?"
"That depends a good deal on where you want to get to," said the cat.
"I don't much care where . . .", said Alice.
"Then it doesn't matter which way you go," said the cat.

Lewis Carroll
Alice in Wonderland

78a guidelines for goalsetting

Once a person has decided where she is, who she is, and where she wants to go, she has identified what success means to her. Now she needs to learn how to establish goals to carry her along the road to success. To set effective goals, it is important that one observe the following guidelines. A goal must be:

1. *Conceivable:* You must be able to conceptualize the goal so that it is understandable and then be able to identify clearly what the first step or two would be.

2. *Believable:* In addition to being consistent with your personal value system, you must believe you can reach the goal. This goes back to the need to have a positive, affirmative feeling about one's self. Bear in mind that few people can believe a goal that they have never seen achieved by someone else. This has serious implications for goal setting in culturally deprived and economically depressed areas.

3. *Achievable:* The goals you set must be accomplishable with your given strengths and abilities. For example, if you were a rather obese forty-five-year-old, it would be foolish for you to set the goal of running a four-minute mile in the next six months—that simply would not be achievable.

4. *Controllable:* If your goal includes the involvement of anyone else, you should first obtain the permission of the other person or persons to be involved; or the goal may be stated as an invitation. For example, if your goal were to take your girlfriend to a movie on Saturday night, the goal would not be acceptable as stated because it involves the possibility that she might turn you down. However, if you said your goal was merely to invite your girlfriend to the movie, it would be acceptable.

5. *Measurable:* Your goal must be stated so that it is measurable in time and quantity. For example, suppose your goal were to work on your term paper this week. You would specify your goal by saying, "I am going to write *twenty pages* by 3:00 P.M. next Monday." That way, the goal can be measured; and when Monday comes, you know whether or not you have achieved it.

6. *Desirable:* Your goal should be something you really want to do. Whatever your ambition, it should be one that you want to fulfill, rather than something you feel you should do. We are well aware that there are many things in life a person has to do, but if he is to be highly motivated, he

must commit a substantial percentage of his time to doing things he wants to do. In other words, there should be a balance in life, but the "want" factor is vital to changing style of being and living.

7. *Stated with No Alternative:* You should set one goal at a time. Our research has shown that a person who says he wants to do one thing or another— giving himself an alternative—seldom gets beyond the "or." He does neither. This does not imply inflexibility. Flexibility in action implies an ability to be able to make a judgment that some action you are involved in is either inappropriate, unnecessary, or the result of a bad decision. Even though you may set out for one goal, you can stop at any time and drop it for a new one. But when you change, you again state your goal without an alternative.

8. *Growth-Facilitating:* Your goal should never be destructive to yourself, to others, or to society. A student recently set a goal to break off fourteen car antennas before 9:00 A.M. the next day. The goal was certainly believable, achievable, measurable, and so forth. Obviously such a goal cannot be supported. If a student is seeking potentially destructive goals, an effort to encourage him to consider a different goal should be made.

Adapted from the work of Dr. Billy B. Sharp

I HAVE A DREAM

I say to you today, my friends, though, even though we face the difficulties of today and tomorrow, I still have a dream. It is a dream deeply rooted in the American dream. I have a dream that one day this nation will rise up, live out the true meaning of its creed: "We hold these truths to be self-evident, that all men are created equal."

I have a dream that one day on the red hills of Georgia sons of former slaves and the sons of former slave-owners will be able to sit down together at the table of brotherhood. I have a dream that one day even the state of Mississippi, a state sweltering with the heat of injustice, sweltering with the heat of oppression, will be transformed into an oasis of freedom and justice.

I have a dream that my four little children will one day live in a nation where they will not be judged by the color of their skin but by the content of their character. I have a dream . . . I have a dream that one day in Alabama, with its vicious racists, with its governor having his lips dripping with the words of interposition and nullification, one day right there in Alabama little black boys and black girls will be able to join hands with little white boys and white girls as sisters and brothers.

I have a dream today . . . I have a dream that one day every valley shall be exalted, every hill and mountain shall be made low. The rough places will be made plain, and the crooked places will be made straight. And the glory of the Lord shall be revealed, and all flesh shall see it together. This is our hope. This is the faith that I go back to the South with. With this faith we will be able to hew out of the mountain of despair a stone of hope. With this faith we will be able to transform the jangling discords of our nation into a beautiful symphony of brotherhood. With this faith we will be able to work together, to stand up for freedom together, knowing that we will be free one day.

Excerpts from Dr. Martin Luther King's
"I Have a Dream" speech, August 28, 1963,
Washington, D.C.

79 I have a dream

Begin this activity by writing *I Have a Dream* on the chalkboard in large letters. Then ask your group, "What dreams do you have?"

About your own development?

About your future?

About your family?

About the world?

Carry on a brief discussion. Perhaps toward the end of the discussion you can share some of your own dreams. At this point, share with them the final paragraphs of Martin Luther King's moving "I Have a Dream" speech given in Washington, D.C., on August 28, 1963. This is one of the most inspiring orations in U.S. history. (A videotape of this and other Dr. King speeches can be purchased from PBS Video, Public Broadcasting Services, 1320 Braddock Place, Alexandria, VA 22314-1698.)

After having read, heard, or seen this beautiful speech by Dr. King, have your group write their own "I Have a Dream" speech. They can each write their own individual speech, or they can collaborate and write one speech for the whole group.

After they have written their speech or speeches, you may want to have them deliver the speeches to the rest of the group, or to another class; or the speeches can be exchanged and read silently. You may want to encourage them to submit their speeches to the school paper or local paper for publication.

Elementary school students can simply list their dreams and perhaps illustrate one or two of them.

> The question is not whether we will be extremist but what kind of extremist will we be. Will we be extremists for hate or will we be extremists for love? Will we be extremists for the preservation of injustice or will we be extremists for the cause of justice?
>
> Dr. Martin Luther King

80 I have a dream—visualization

This activity follows the previous exercise wherein students identify dreams they have about themselves, their school, family, or world.

Ask them to select the one dream they consider most important and, in groups of four, to share that dream.

When everyone is done sharing but students are still in their groups, ask them to close their eyes and become very relaxed and quiet. Guide them in the following visualization:

> I'd like you to visualize (picture in your mind) having achieved your dream. See it as already accomplished. Use all of your senses as you visualize your success—in other words, pay attention to what you see, hear, smell, feel, taste, or touch. Notice the reactions of others. Notice how you feel about your accomplishment. Are you smiling? Happy? Energized? What are you thinking? What are you saying? What are you doing? Stay with your visualization by noticing who is with you, what they're saying. What is your life like now? How does the world seem? Are others joining and supporting you in your work? Who are they? How are they helping? Develop your visualization for a couple of minutes on your own.

After a suitable length of time, tell them to gradually bring their visualizations to a conclusion. Have the students share their visualizations in their small groups.

It is also helpful for students to write a description of what they visualized. This reinforces the experience and help them retain it.

This visualization activity is designed to let young people "experience" a major success in advance, thus encouraging them to take the necessary concrete steps to succeed. For some people, being persistent in the pursuit of their goals is at least as difficult as getting started. Teaching them to visualize periodically the successful accomplishment of their desires helps. For the best results, ask the students to visualize their goals as already achieved twice a day. The two best times are just upon waking and right before going to sleep at night.

81 I have a dream—making it happen

It is one thing to have dreams and another to accomplish them. Obviously, most dreams as goals can't be accomplished immediately. People are still working on Martin Luther King's dreams, as they no doubt will have to do for many years to come. Yet Dr. King took specific steps to help realize his dreams, as we all must do with ours if they are to become reality.

Share these thoughts with your students. Then have them individually write down three actual things they can do to move toward the realization of one of their dreams. These must be concrete steps, behaviors that are observable and can be tabulated or recorded as discrete occurrences. Have them attach a time to these behaviors; that is, specifically when are they going to start? How often are they going to do the behavior? Where are they going to keep track of their efforts and their progress? The pupil's journals (see Exercise 1) may be good places for recording efforts. Example:

> *Tomorrow, Tuesday, March 16, after school, I will talk to the librarian about where to find information on the Peace Corps.*
> *Wednesday, after school, I will write the Peace Corps for information on qualifications and sites and ask for an applications.*
> *When I receive the Peace Corps information, I will immediately discuss the material with my school counselor.*

Sometimes a chart where students can record specific behaviors is helpful.

When the group has given sufficient attention to these questions—that is, has done some actual planning— have them pair up to share and help one another further refine their planning.

We like William Glasser's ideas of:

1. Having the students *sign* a personalized written contract that they will undertake the pursuit of their goal as they've outlined it.

2. Not punishing or reprimanding those who fall short. Simply ask again if this is a goal they wish to pursue. If so, help get them back on track.

Make sure to provide a time for regular feedback on where they are with respect to their goals as time goes on.

Nothing is impossible to a willing heart.

English proverb

82 on course/off course—a guidance system

Explain to the class that the world gives us feedback all the time. This feedback lets us know whether we are on course or off course—whether we are accomplishing our goals or not. This is called *external feedback*. *Internal feedback* is something we give ourselves, which also lets us know if we're on track or not.

External "on-course" feedback can be getting an "A" on a test, having others appreciate us for a job well done or accomplishing a task successfully. Internal "on-course" feedback is feeling good about ourselves, rejoicing in a job well done, or feeling proud for rejecting peer pressure.

External "off-course" feedback can be getting a "D" or an "F" on a test or receiving complaints about a job we did or didn't do. Internal "off-course" feedback can be having a headache at the end of the day, feeling nauseous before a test, or being unhappy or depressed.

To illustrate how feedback works, select a student to be the "feedback mechanism." Direct the student in the following way:

> *What I want you to do is stand across the room so that you are directly opposite of me . . . Good. You are my goal. My job is to get to you. You will also be my feedback mechanism. Your job is to provide a constant stream of feedback like a broken record. You will say "on course" every time I move in a straight line directly toward you. You will say "off course" if I do anything else. Clear? . . . O.K., ready? Begin . . . (pause) . . .*

Do not move. Just stand there. The student will begin the steady stream of feedback but will peter out after a few seconds. Ask: "Why did you stop?" Invariably, the answer will be, "Because you weren't moving." At which point say to the class:

> *Aha! Lesson number one. The universe only responds to action! If you want feedback, you have to do something—anything! Many people don't do anything productive toward their goals: they just hope for something to happen. So lesson number one is do something!*
>
> *O.K., [volunteer], let's do this again.*

With your first step, the student should begin a steady stream of "on course—off course." This time, move slowly toward the student in a zigzag fashion, making sure you are off course more of the time than on course. When you reach the student (your "goal"), turn to the class and ask: "Was I 'on course' or 'off course' more of the time?" They will respond, "Off course!" You respond: "Did I reach my goal?" They will answer, "Yes." Say:

> *Remember that! I was off course most of the time, but I still reached my goal. The object is to complete a task successfully, not avoid errors along the way. In doing anything the first, second, or even third time, people make mistakes. That's how they learn. There is no such thing as failure: there is only a delay in results.*

Say, "Let me now show you some ineffective ways people deal with feedback."

THE FREAKOUT

Move toward the volunteer student who is providing feedback. Veer off course and continue off course even though the student says, "Off course." Instead of correcting your movements, "freak out," throwing your arms into the air and screaming, "ARRRRGH! I can't take it any more. It's just too *hard!* Waaaaa!" Ask the class: "Do any of you handle feedback in this manner—by falling apart?"

ATTACK THE SOURCE OF THE FEEDBACK

Move toward the student providing feedback. Veer off course and continue off course. Instead of correcting your movements, stop, put your hands on your hips and yell at the student, "Complain, complain, complain! Is that all you ever do? Don't you ever say anything nice?" Ask the class: "Do any of you ever react to corrective suggestions in this way—by getting angry?"

"I DON'T CARE WHAT YOU SAY, I'M RIGHT!"

Move toward the student providing feedback. Veer off course. Instead of correcting your movement, plug both your ears with your fingers and continue in the wrong direction. Ask the students: "Do any of you ignore the signs that say you are heading in the wrong direction? Do you ever continue to make mistakes rather than take corrective measures? Do you shut out parents, teachers, coaches, and friends who are trying to assist you?"

THE MOST EFFECTIVE WAY TO USE FEEDBACK

This time, move toward the student providing feedback deliberately, slowly, one step at a time. Veer off course, and as soon as the student says, "off course," immediately stop. Tentatively put one foot out in several different "off course" directions, but without forward movement. Then place your foot directly "on course," hear the feedback, and continue slowly, deliberately forward.

Continue the process of going off course/listening and testing/moving on course until you reach the student. Have students discuss what they have seen. Point out that the most efficient way to reach a goal is to listen to the feedback you are getting and to correct any off-course behavior.

83  five years ahead: resume

FIVE YEARS AHEAD

After each student has engaged in the "Strength Bombardment" exercise (see Exercise 38), ask him to fantasize for himself or for another what kind of person he would be and what he would be doing five years from now if he fully developed and used all the strengths he identified in himself. Then ask him to write in his journal a description of that person (five years from now, with his strengths fully developed) and what his life is like.

We learned this exercise from Dr. Billy Sharp.

RESUME

Explain to the students the function of a resume in job seeking. If you have a copy of a resume available, share it with your students. Brainstorm with the students some possible categories (scholastic achievements, hobbies, athletic successes, skills they have attained, jobs they have held, etc.) they could use in creating a resume for themselves. Then ask them to imagine a job they would like to hold. Have them share their choices with the class. Ask them to list their past accomplishments, personal strengths, and skills they have that they would "sell" to their prospective employer or interviewer in order to secure the job. Have them create a resume and role-play a job interview.

The idea for this exercise came from Audrey Peterson.

> The idea expressed in the Biblical "love thy neighbor as thyself!" implies that respect for one's own integrity and uniqueness, love for and understanding for one's own self, cannot be separated from respect and love and understanding for another individual. The love for my own self is inseparably connected with love for any other being.
>
> Erich Fromm
> *The Art of Loving*

84 the six o'clock news

Have participants write a TV news report beginning with a dateline and telling something that the writer might do in the future. In other words, the six o'clock news becomes a kind of "hoped for" autobiography.

The newscast should elaborate briefly on the major events of the writer's "proposed" life.

When these are completed, set up the room as an informal TV newscast studio with four or five participants, each in turn reading her autobiographical human interest news item. For example:

> *January 7, 1996*
> *A TV 8 exclusive!*
> *Yesterday, a young American woman named Maria Gonzalez was elected president of Mexico. Ms. Gonzalez is the first U.S. citizen to be elected president of another nation and also the first non-Mexican to be elected to major office in that country.*
>
> *Ms. Gonzalez's climb from obscurity in Chicago to prominence in world politics is almost unbelievable. Her early professional career was teaching. She had taught at the high school and university levels before moving to Mexico to help develop that country's economy.*
>
> *In 1995, she was awarded the Nobel Peace Prize.*

the language of self

The field of general semantics has made an important contribution to the self-esteem movement. Some teachers have been particularly skilled in applying general semantics principles to the classroom situation in order to build an affective environment and create intrapersonal awareness.

It is certainly well known that our language effects our thinking. For example, we often say somebody "is" something. Our thinking is thereby conditioned to accept the notion that whatever the quality "is," it sure enough resides in the person! In truth however, to say that somebody "is" something only means that *the speaker attributes* that quality to the person. Quite a difference!

This section, "The Language of Self," is composed primarily of activities that have a general semantics base. However, Three important new exercises have been added to build on the previous offerings.

> We can do no great things—only small things with great love.
>
> Mother Teresa
> *Quotable Woman*

85 reframing hurtful assumptions

Reframing is a powerful tool used by educators, counselors, and therapists. This simple concept is not easy to practice. *Reframing*, simply defined, means converting negative, self-defeating thinking about an event into a more positive point of view. It is just as likely that the positive interpretation of the stimulus event is true as is the negative one. For example:

A man meets for the first time a woman from the same city. The woman says, "Oh, yes, I've seen you around town," to which the man replies, "Really? I don't believe I've ever seen you." The woman thinks to herself, "Oh my, I seem to be an invisible person," or, "I must be terribly plain never to be noticed." She may go on with a litany of self-pitying, self-defeating thoughts. However, the man's declaration is open to several equally valid interpretations.

1. He may have seen her, thought her attractive, but forgotten the encounter.

2. He may be a singularly unobservant man.

Realizing that other interpretations are possible, the woman can choose to think positively: "Well, isn't it interesting that I'm so much more observant than he is." Or, "I wonder if my scientific training is what enables me to observe what goes on around me." Or, "I look great tonight! I bet he'll remember me from now on." Each of these latter interpretations enhances her self-esteem, whereas the first set of assumptions lowers her self-esteem. Another illustration:

A junior high girl knows that an acquaintance is having a slumber party, and that she has not been invited. She assumes that the acquaintance doesn't like her and carries on a line of negative thinking (see "Whack the Vulture" on page 229). Some other possible interpretations she might consider include:

1. The party giver's mother may have specified only three girls were to be invited; or

2. The party giver may have known that her acquaintance frequently visited a relative in another city on weekends; or

3. The girl not invited might have mentioned disliking slumber parties at some time in the past, or that she didn't enjoy being with the party giver's best friend.

In other words, *there is no reason to assume something negative about either the party giver or the uninvited one in this instance.*

Students can be taught to rethink their negative interpretations of events, with a view to enhancing their own esteem. Presenting them with a few examples similar to that provided above is a first step. Examples may be drawn from students' or your own life experiences.

A next step will be to note the all-too-frequent occasions when students criticize one another, and ask them for alternative approaches to the stimulus situation or request that they change a negative interpretation into one that enhances their self-esteem.

Third, students can learn to help one another—a form of peer counseling. Have the students write about an event in their lives about which they have beaten themselves up with a negative analysis or interpretation. In pairs, students can explore alternative ways to reframe their thinking about the events they have chosen.

> The meaning of an event always resides in the individual, not the event itself. Human beings are meaning creators. Ten people can have the same experience, but it can have significantly different meaning for each of them.
>
> Harold Clive Wells

86 words that describe me

Ask your students to write down three words that describe themselves. Given thoughtful attention, any three words that come to mind are appropriate. They can be descriptive of physical, emotional, mental, personality or character traits.

When they have done that, ask them to turn the paper over and write three words they *wish* described themselves.

Now have each person take one of the three words on his second list and describe *specific* behaviors that that kind of person exhibits. For example, Charlie says, "I want to be kind." What specific behaviors do "kind" people exhibit?

They help people in distress:

Take food to someone who is hungry

Mow the lawn for a neighbor who is injured or ill

Baby-sit temporarily for a working mother while she finds a replacement for a "permanent" sitter who quit

What else do "kind" people do?

They are considerate of others' feelings:

Sally says, "I hate doing the dishes!" A kind person may respond, "Let me help you."

Billy spills milk on the floor and Ben says, "Billy, you sure are clumsy!" A kind person might retort, "No, he's not clumsy; he simply spilled his milk!"

Your class will need some help being specific enough to do any good, so give some examples on the board using words from a couple of students' lists.

When each student has completed listing specific behaviors for one of his words, ask him to use that word as a goal. Use the behaviors as some suggested ways of meeting that goal. If Charlie wants to be "kind," he can immediately start to practice some of the behaviors he has listed and can begin to look for other opportunities as well.

This exercise develops self-esteem only if people work at doing something about their goal. You can help assure this by having a five-minute session once a week in which students state their goals and give examples of something they've done to help accomplish them.

"I have hairy arms, one wart on my pinky finger, kitten scratches all over my hands, red lips and a small nose."

Lawrence Branagan and Christopher Moroney

87

I am not my description

In the previous activity, students were asked to write three words that described themselves. Many people, given such an opportunity, write words that are negative in connotation. For example, one young boy wrote: "bad; I fight; dumb."

The trouble starts when we assume that labels like "bad" and "dumb" are actually us! These self-labels are repeated by us over and over until they affect our every action. Repeated internally for years, they have the cumulative effect of being terribly self-crippling.

Use the negative words that your students wrote in the previous exercise or ask them to write down two "bad" things about themselves. Pick them up and list all the items on a large sheet of paper (you'll want to save it for the next activity).

Discuss the items listed in reference to their reality (don't identify the writer). "Are you *always* 'bad'?" "Under what circumstances are you 'bad'?" Help your class through this discussion to realize that what they considered as "bad" characteristics are nothing more (or less) than labels they've applied to certain kinds of behavior that occurred in particular situations in the past. There is no point in applying those labels to their present situations and certainly not to the future.

Show them how to rewrite their "bad" words to make them more realistic, more scientific, and less damaging to themselves. This involves writing about specific behaviors, specific times, in specific situations. An illustration might be: "Yesterday I hit a boy" (rather than "I'm bad" or "I fight a lot") or "I haven't learned to multiply by 8's or 9's (rather than "I'm dumb about arithmetic."). Notice that the rewritten sentences do not imply worthlessness in the present or hopelessness for the future. Now have them rewrite their words.

As an assignment, have your students keep track for a day of every time they tell themselves they are "bad" (*or act as if* they were).

Follow this up with a class discussion.

> Whatever one believes to be true either is true or becomes true in one's mind.
> John C. Lilly
> *The Center of the Cyclone*

88 the tyranny of "should"

This is a follow-up to the previous activity. Use the same words, if possible.

Many of the words your students used to describe "bad" things about themselves implied that they *should* or *ought to* be this or that. For example, some kids are apt to say, "I'm ugly," or "I'm fat," or "I'm afraid." All these words imply that they should be the opposite: "I should be beautiful!"; "I ought to be thin!;" or "I should be brave!" Several things are wrong here but we'll deal with only one and save another for the next activity.

Who says everybody *ought* to look like a movie or TV star, and that anyone who looks very different from that general conception of beauty is ugly? Who says we all *should* be brave or thin? These are culturally induced values that may or may not be appropriate to specific situations. The fantastic psychological damage that has been done to most of us by our *believing* the Hollywood conception of beauty is inestimable. So it is with numerous other values that we derive from our society. Our mental health can be improved by understanding that "should" and "ought to," when applied indiscriminately to culturally induced values are, in fact, prejudicial—because we believe in advance that we *should* look or behave in certain ways, and consequently we do not view each new event as a fresh experience to feel about and react to as we naturally would, but instead spend our time anxiously concerned with "shoulds" and "oughts."

When you've discussed this idea with your class, have them form small groups of six to eight people. Their task is to list as many examples as they can of things we *should* believe according to our culture. For example:

It is "good" to work.

It is "good" to own many things.

Blondes have more fun.

If you are a man working in an office, you "should" wear a tie.

Everyone "ought" to be a good reader.

When the groups are done, list their contributions on the chalkboard and discuss them.

Have each individual write a page about his two "bad" things in which he tells why it is damaging to him to continue to believe that he *ought to or should* (whatever they are).

> If you have made mistakes . . . there is always another chance for you . . . You may have a fresh start any moment you choose, for this thing we call "failure" is not the falling down, but the staying down.
>
> Mary Pickford
> *Quotable Woman*

89 scientific language

There is another simple idea from the field of general semantics that you can teach your students to help them get a better perspective on the "bad" things about themselves. Use the same list of words or phrases you compiled from the previous two or three activities.

We often attribute value to something as though only two value choices existed–things are assumed to be good or bad, white or black, dirty or clean, right or wrong, etc.

Take some of the "bad" things your pupils wrote about themselves. Notice how often they imply a two-valued system as they say, "I am bad" as though there were only two alternatives. Point out to them that even such terribly abstract concepts as good and bad fall on a continuum—a line with "good" at one end and "bad" on the other; and that an enormous range of behaviors can be classified along the line, some "better" or "worse" than others.

Take the list of words your students gave you, pick out a couple that illustrate this point, and talk to your class about them. Draw a continuum using one of their words or phrases. Discuss various points on the continuum to show how opposites blend together as there are degrees of "badness" and "goodness" or whatever it is you are using as concepts.

At this point, if you've followed this sequence of three lessons, your students should realize that (1) they often label themselves as if they always were and always will be their label, (2) they often make themselves unhappy by believing they should be some idealized image they've learned from society, and (3) they are frequently victims of two-valued logic (things are either one thing or its opposite).

Break your class into groups of four and assign each group the task of developing a small play or skit that illustrates these ideas. They should perform both the unscientific and scientific ways of dealing with these concepts.

> The most immutable barrier in nature is between one man's thoughts and another's.
>
> William James

© 1992 Watterson/Distributed by Universal Press Syndicate

90 volunteering

An interesting and profitable exercise for many people is this simple imagination technique. As the leader, you suggest to the group that you're going to ask for a volunteer in a couple of minutes to do "something in front of the group." Pause for a considerable time and then proceed by saying something like, "I don't think you'll find it embarrassing to do, but it may take someone with quite a bit of nerve to be up here." Again pause. If someone volunteers, just ignore that person. Again proceed, "Well, I'm sure you want to know more before you volunteer, but I'd prefer not to reveal any more at this moment." Pause again.

Now smile and say you've just been putting them on—you don't really want a volunteer. Notice the reaction of relief! Have the group discuss their feelings about volunteering. How many were prepared to volunteer? Some people will resent the put-on. Deal with that but don't let it sidetrack the "to volunteer or not" issue.

When you've discussed these things for a few minutes, have everyone close their eyes and imagine two selves, one a volunteering self and the other a nonvolunteering self. Have these two imaginative characters engage in a dialogue in each participant's mind. After three or four minutes of quiet for the fantasy exercise, invite the group to share what their characters were saying.

Ask, "Which won the argument, your volunteering or nonvolunteering self? What arguments were used by the winner? Did you use these same arguments when you were considering my request for a volunteer? To what extent do you say negative things about yourself because you don't like to be the center of attraction? How is your self-concept affected by these kinds of statements?"

> Imagination was given to man to compensate him for what he is not. A sense of humor was provided to console him for what he is.
>
> Horace Walpole

Rubes®

By Leigh Rubin

8-25

"I don't know, what do you think we should do ...
have a funeral or a picnic?"

91 whack the vulture

In the previous exercise, "Volunteering," participants had a chance to see how quickly and easily most of them fell into negative self-talk. THE VULTURE LURKS WITHIN! Every time a person says, "I can't," "I'm dumb," "I don't know," "I'm afraid," "Someone hates me," it's the internal vulture feasting, tearing away pieces of self-respect and self-confidence. Discuss this with your elementary or middle school youngsters.

Ask them for more examples of negative messages they give themselves, and record them on the board.

Then discuss the term *monitor*. * Tell them they can monitor their self-talk. Perhaps they can create a picture of a *Vulture Monitor*.

Explain that after they recognize the Vulture, they must whack him by replacing negative self-talk with positive self-talk.

Using the negative examples on the board, see if they can come up with counteracting sentences. For example:

> *Vulture:* Geez, am I ever stupid!
>
> *Vulture Monitor:* Oh, oh, negative self-talk!
>
> *Vulture:* Wow, this test is hard. I'll probably flunk it!
>
> *Vulture Monitor:* Watch it!
>
> *Vulture Whacker:* Even though it's a hard test, I can remember quite a few things; I'll do those first and surprise myself at how much I do know; then maybe the rest won't seem so bad.

Perhaps someone can draw or find a large picture of a vulture that can be displayed in the room, with the caption THE VULTURE LURKS WITHIN!

When you hear someone's Vulture at work, remind him or her of the need to Whack the Vulture and perhaps help supply a positive self-talk statement.

---

* *Monitor:* (verb): to watch or check on a person or thing; to regulate the performance of.

148,000 "NO'S!"

During the first eighteen years of our lives, if we grew up in fairly average, reasonably positive homes, we were told "No!," or what we could *not* do, more than *148,000 times!* If you were a little more fortunate, you may have been told "No!" only 100,000 times, or 50,000 times—however many, it was considerably more negative programming than any of us needs.

Shad Helmstetter, Ph.D.
What to Say When You Talk to Yourself

92 I can't . . . I won't

Ask the students to find partners. Have them take turns saying sentences that start with the words "I can't . . ." Ask them to consider their school life, their social life, their home life, etc., as possible areas from which to draw these true statements.

After about four or five minutes, ask them to go back and repeat all the sentences they have just said with one change: replacing the word *can't* with the word *won't* or *I don't want to.* Explain to them that the words "I won't" may not feel right to them the first time they say them, but that it is like going into a clothing store and trying on a coat. It may not fit you, but you won't know that until you try it on. Just because you say it, doesn't mean you are stuck with it forever. It is simply an experiment to discover how we experience ourselves differently after saying "I won't" instead of "I can't."

Ask them to repeat exactly what they said before except for the substitution of *won't* for *can't,* and to take the time to be aware of how they experience saying each sentence. Again, give them about five minutes to do this.

Bring the class back together and ask them what they experienced as they did the exercise. Did they experience any difference between saying "I can't" and "I won't?" Usually responses will include such statements as:

I felt more powerful when I said, "I won't!"

I felt like "I can't" was a cop out.

I felt like I was more in charge with "I won't."

When I said "I can't," it was as if there was some outside force controlling me. With "I won't" I realized that the decision to do it or not to do it was all in me.

I sounded whiney when I said, "I can't."

"I won't" sounded more true to me.

"I won't" made me feel more responsible.

Ask them to consider whether their "I can't" statements are really statements of something that is impossible, or whether it is something possible that they simply refuse to do. Ask them to become aware of and to affirm their power of refusal. "I can't" implies being unable, crippled, and controlled from the outside. "I won't" affirms the responsibility for their actions. Often this reaffirmation of responsibility even leads to the transformation of an "I can't" to an "I will."

After you have used this exercise with your class, make a habit of correcting people in class who say "I can't." Ask them to repeat whatever they have said with the words "I won't."

93 please . . . no!; . . . yes . . . no!

A student-teacher introduced us to this little dialogue game, which turned out to be valuable for some of our pupils.

Pair up your class or group and have them decide which of them will be A and which B. Stop the process right here and ask them to examine and discuss with one another how the choice of who was A and who was B was made. "Is there a pattern in your life that is exemplified by your taking the lead and deciding which letter you would be? Is it typical of you to let someone else decide such matters? If your partner had been of the opposite sex from what he or she is, would that have affected how your letter would have been chosen? Think about it!"

Now go back to your original activity. Have the A's take the part of the please-sayer; the B's each time are to respond with "No!" Keep this up, one saying "Please" and the other "No!" until the no-sayer (B) feels that the pleader has reached a deep sense of sincerity and humility in his request. Then he responds with "Yes!"

Have the partners change roles. Obviously there is no particular subject matter for the "please" request. Each player may make whatever assumptions he wishes about it, but the "thing" is not to be decided upon.

One of our students revealed that she couldn't play the part of the please-sayer. She said, "I've always got to be on top." That was an insightful and honest confrontation with herself and the class and the moment was treated in such an accepting way as to justify her trust in our understanding.

A variation of this exercise is to have the A's say "Yes!" and the B's respond with "No!" Let it develop into a lively two-word conversation using only the words "yes" and "no." Learning to say "No!" is very important—if they don't learn to say it, people may allow themselves to be walked over by other people's expectations and desires. In reality a real "yes" cannot exist without the ability to say "no." If one is not able to say "no" with a straight face and mean it, then his "yes" is no more than a conditioned reflex action.

> I want you to feel like loving your opponent, and the way to do it is to give them the same credit for honesty of purpose which you would claim for yourself.
>
> Gandhi

94 incredible affirmations

Monitoring self-talk and "Whacking the Vulture" (see Exercise 91) help students retain and strengthen their self-esteem by dealing with negativity as it occurs. Another approach is to create positive self-talk in advance and repeat it frequently. This positive self-talk is called an *affirmation.* An affirmation asserts a desired condition or objective as though it were already a reality—for example, "My speech is so good I deserve a standing ovation!"

An affirmation has six basic ingredients: It's personal, it's positive, it's specific, it's visual, it's present tense, and it's emotional.

Here are some additional affirmations to give you the idea:

"I enjoy being kind and compassionate with my students."

"I am proudly accepting the Most Valuable Player Award at the school assembly."

"I am happily learning my algebra easily and well."

Affirmations work best if they come out of visualizing a desired objective.

1. Ask the students to visualize a goal. It might be a desired character or personality attribute or a school or career goal. Ask them to place themselves in the visualized picture.

2. Ask them to hear the sounds they would hear if everything were happening the way they want it to.

3. Ask them to feel and experience the emotions they will feel when this goal is achieved.

4. Have them begin to create an affirmation by describing what they are feeling and doing, as if they were telling someone else—that is, "I am excitedly telling my mother that I got an 'A' in science!"

5. Now, have your group record their affirmations and edit them to fit the guidelines above. Members can share with a buddy or two for help in creating exactly what they intended.

6. Have cards ready for recording affirmations to be carried in notebooks or wallets, where they will be seen frequently. Suggest that the way to keep their visualizations and affirmations fresh and effective is to repeat them a minimum of twice a day.

"I like my room the best of
all my inside places because off of my
closet there is a little attic room that
is all mine."

Lawrence Branagan and Christopher Moroney

95 identity, connectedness, and power

In their book *Toward Humanistic Education: A Curriculum of Affect*, Gerald Weinstein and Mario Fantini suggest that there are three areas of concern that people seem to spend most of their time thinking about:

> *Identity* basically deals with the question "Who am I?" Various forms of this question are: Why am I a girl? Why was I born black? What do I really feel about things? How come I act the way I do? How come I'm in the dumb class? What's really important in life? What can I do to be more happy?

> *Connectedness* deals with the issue of my relationships with others in my world. Typical concerns from this area are: Who are my friends? What are my values? To whom do I owe my allegiance? How do I make new friends? What do I want from other people? What am I willing to give up of myself to get what I want from others?

> *Power* refers to the sense of control over one's own life. Typical expressions about one's concern with power are: I can do anything I set my mind to! Why should I even try; nothing ever works out the way I want it to. I don't have a chance, man; I have to do what they say. How can I get a good job with a "C" average?

What we've done below is to list more incomplete sentences similar to those in previous exercises, only this time we have divided them into the three areas of identity, connectedness, and power. Most of these have been brainstormed by teachers who have been in our training workshops. A group of five teachers can usually generate over fifty sentence stubs in a period of five or six minutes. So, when you run out of these, get together with some other teachers and invent some more. It's easy—and useful.

IDENTITY

My favorite . . . is . . .

If I could have one wish, it would be . . .
I'm happiest when I . . .
I feel the saddest when . . .
I feel most important when I . . .

One question I have about life is . . .
I get angry when . . .

A fantasy I enjoy is . . .
A thought I keep having is . . .
When I get angry I . . .

When I feel sad I . . .

When I feel scared I . . .

I get scared when . . .
Something I want but I'm afraid to
ask for is . . .
I feel brave when . . .
I felt brave when . . .
I love to . . .

I see myself as . . .
Something I do well is . . .
I worry about my . . .
My greatest asset is . . .
I often think about . . .

More than anything else, I would
like to . . .
If I were an adult I would . . .
If I were a little kid I would . . .

The best thing about being me
is . . .
The worst thing about being me
is . . .
I hate . . .
I need . . .

I wonder about . . .
I bet . . .
I feel like my mother/father
when . . .
I do my best work when . . .
My body is . . .
My face is . . .
I feel uncomfortable when . . .
The thing I'm most afraid to talk
about is . . .
I don't want to . . .

I am afraid to . . .
I wish I had the courage to . . .

CONNECTEDNESS

People are . . .
My friends are . . .
The thing that makes me a good
friend is . . .
The things I look for in a friend
are . . .
My parents . . .
My brother(s)/sister(s) . . .
Other people make me feel . . .
Older people are . . .
Younger people are . . .
I wish people would . . .
I wish my family would . . .
I like people who . . .
I don't like people who . . .
I believe . . .
I value . . .
I make friends by . . .

Girls . . .
Boys . . .
People can get to me by . . .
Teasing people is . . .
When people tease me I . . .
When someone tells me they like
me, I . . .
People like me because . . .
People think I am . . .
I think I am . . .
Someone I'd like to get to know
better is . . .
Something I do for my mother
is . . .
Something I do for my father is . . .
I like it when somebody says to
me . . .
I wish I had told . . .

My best friend . . .
My teacher . . .
I wish my teacher would . . .
The other students in this class . . .

I stop myself from talking in class by
imagining that . . .
I resent . . . for . . .
I appreciate . . .
I demand . . .
I pretend to be . . . when I'm
really . . .

POWER

Something I do well is . . .
Something I'm getting better at
is . . .
I can . . .
I am proud that I . . .
I get people's attention by . . .
I get my way by . . .
My greatest strength is . . .
I can help other people to . . .
I taught someone how to . . .
I need help on . . .
I'm learning to . . .
I feel big when . . .
I have the power to . . .
I was able to devide to . . .
When people try to boss me around
I . . .
I don't like people to help me
with . . .
Something I can do all by myself
is . . .
People can't make me . . .
I got into trouble when I . . .

I get praise from others when I . . .
The most powerful person I know
is . . .
People seem to respect me when
I . . .
I want to be able to . . .
I want to be strong enough to . . .
A time when I was a leader was . . .
I'm not afraid to . . .
Something that I can do now that I
couldn't do last year is . . .
When I want my parents to do
something I . . .
I have difficulty dealing with . . .
People who expect a lot from me
make me feel . . .
I have accomplished . . .
If I want to, I can . . .
People who agree with me make me
feel . . .
Strong independent people . . .
If I were the teacher I would . . .

"My mother and father are very kind. I like them very much."

Lawrence Branagan and Christopher Moroney

240

seven

relationships with others

It is a truism that self-love precedes love of others. Hence, we have concentrated on *self*-awareness, *self*-identity, and *self*-esteem, knowing that these are prerequisites to loving others. It seems appropriate, then, that our *final* section deals with "relationships with others."

We achieve our sense of self, our identity, in and through relationships. One thinks immediately of poet John Donne's "No Man Is an Island".

The quest for self-actualization has never meant the development of the self in isolation or at the expense of others. There *is* no self without others. So, in this section we pay particular attention to students' relationships to family, friends, and peers—those most influential in their development.

> Our study indicated that once people become involved in healthy, helping acts, they experience strong benefits and therefore are motivated to help all the more. Their empathy for others, for strangers, grows, and their health improves.
>
> Allan Luks
> *The Healing Power of Doing Good*

96 the family

The dynamics and relationships of the family are constant sources of confusion for children. Here are several exercises designed to help children explore and accept their feelings about their families.

Ask the students to describe their feelings about their older and younger sisters and brothers. Include stepsisters and stepbrothers, half-brothers, etc. Be sensitive to the many different family systems that currently exist. Recount some of your own experiences to the children first.

Ask the students who have brothers or sisters to write an essay describing their relationship(s) with them. The students who are only children may write on the topic: "Why I would like to have a brother or sister." It is always an enlightening experience to have the children compare the two types of papers.

Have students write about a situation in which the members of their families showed kindness and understanding toward one another.

Give them the opportunity to talk or write about what it would be like to be an orphan.

Ask each child to write a composition describing how each member of her family, including herself, is unique and different. How do these differences contribute to a stronger family?

Using the voting technique described in Exercise 48, ask the students the following questions:

How many of you like one parent more than the other?

How many of you have no father living at home? No mother living at home?

How many of you have ever wished that one of your family would go away and stay away?

How many of you have ever wished that you were dead?

How many of you wish you were the father or mother?

How many of you have ever disliked your mother, if only for a moment?

How many of you have ever disliked your father, if only for a moment?

Did you notice how many other people had the same feelings as you? It is quite normal to sometimes dislike or hate the people you love. It is also quite normal not to love everybody the same.

Be aware that some students may have experienced emotional, physical and/or sexual abuse from family members. Be prepared for these kinds of revelations to surface. If you feel unprepared to deal with these feelings, refer the student to a qualified counselor.

GOOD-BYE

I said goodbye
As you left for good
Why didn't you say good-bye?

You had tears in your eyes
Your smile wiped them away.

You laid in that hospital bed
Not looking at me at all
Did you do that on purpose?

I felt alone
Because you never talked to me
Weren't you glad I was there?

The nurses rushed in and out
You never answered one
question of theirs.

You still had time to tell me
good-bye as you drifted off
So why did you close
your eyes and leave me?

I had tears streaming down
my cheeks
You touched my hand and
that was it
Was that good-bye to you?

I was mad at you and
You didn't care
I yelled and you
Just kept your eyes
on that ceiling.

If you were mad at me why
didn't you tell me?
Maybe it would've helped if I
changed my ways.

I never expressed my feelings or
complimented you
I'm sorry.

I'll never know why you kept
your eyes on that ceiling
I am really sorry.

It's too late to say sorry now
The truth is, it's not too late
to change my ways.

by Sheri Pavvoski
Mrs. Bynum's fifth-grade class
Buckley Michigan Community School

97 making friends

Making friends and staying friends are two of a young person's major concerns.

We've long been intrigued by the work of sociologist Pitirim Sorokin at Harvard University, where he organized and directed the Center for Creative Altruism.

Sorokin asked his Harvard students to name their worst enemies. He then directed them to find something they could sincerely do for those enemies. Amazingly, in over 75 percent of the cases, doing a simple act of unselfishness for an "enemy" turned the enemy into a friend!

Share this information with your class and discuss it. Then ask students to write down secretly the name of a person whom they'd like to have as a friend (someone in their real life—not a movie or TV star).

Brainstorm in class the kinds of things they might do for others that would be sincere and appreciated. This is not an attempt to "buy" a friend. It's putting oneself out for another person. It is the essence of friendship.

Tell them you're going to follow up tomorrow and on a regular basis to see how they're progressing. In subsequent sessions, help them over the rough spots, particularly the question of what they can do for their target "friend."

At the conclusion (in a week or two) of this effort, ask the students to generalize about what they've learned about themselves and about relationships.

It is possible to coach children in the art of being likable. One study showed that individual coaching sessions can produce long-term improvements in popularity.

Robert M. Leibert
The Child

I'm a stranger
   Don't drive me away
I'm a stranger
   Don't drive me away
If you drive me away
   You may need me some day
I'm a stranger
   Don't drive me away . . .

A hymn quoted in *12 Million*
                Black Voices

Perhaps a child who is fussed over gets a feeling of destiny; he thinks he is in the world for something important and it gives him drive and confidence.

Dr. Benjamin Spock

 **love notes**

In the first book we wrote back in 1970, entitled *About Me,* we included a feature in the Teachers' Guide called "Love Notes to a Teacher."[1] These were sprinkled throughout the Guide to give a lift to the instructor and a teaching tip as well. For example, one read:

LOVE NOTE TO A TEACHER

One reason we love teachers is that they are so conscious of kids' needs for support. Special thanks for noticing the needs of new kids in school.

Letter writing may be a chore in busy schedules, but a quick, informal note can brighten a day significantly. Perhaps we can help students begin a lifetime habit of writing "love notes."

Tell your class what you're going to have them do and explain why. Then have them think for a few minutes about a person in their lives who has been especially important, or who has recently done something they think should be acknowledged, perhaps a person whom they think could really use a morale boost right now. This is a wonderful way for you to encourage children to reach out, to strengthen their empathy for others.

Have them jot a brief note of appreciation/validation to their chosen person and make plans for the notes to be delivered or mailed.

While the students are writing their notes, we urge you to be writing one as well—maybe even a "Love Note to My Class" to be posted on the bulletin board.

Some "Love Note" sessions can be structured to be directed to specific subjects (targets). The following will give you some ideas:

Love note to myself

. . . to the principal

. . . to the school custodian

---

[1] Harold C. Wells with Jack Canfield, *About Me, A Teacher's Guide and Student Book* (Chicago: Encyclopedia Britannica Educational Corporation, 1970). (Out of print.)

   . . . to another class

   . . . to grandparents

   . . . to brothers and/or sisters

LOVE NOTE TO YOU, OUR READER

We really want you to know how exciting and rewarding you make our lives. We just can't get over what dedication and commitment and love you bring to your students and your profession. God bless you!

Harold and Jack

 **class applause**

The class applause exercise is a simple technique for cheering up a fellow class member. (It works for staff members too!) Often a student indicates frustration, discouragement, or some other feeling or behavior that lets you know he is "down." Sometimes you can sense that someone needs support; other times you might simply ask if there is anyone that would like a lift.

When a candidate for class applause has been identified, have everyone jump to their feet, clap their hands, and shout words of encouragement and affection for the "down" person. The applauders may hug or pat the recipient on the back to give further strength to the response.

Obviously this exercise can be futile or phoney if done insincerely or at the wrong time—but it can also lead to demonstrated caring for one's fellow class members. At other times it may be more efficacious to spend some time allowing the target person to simply talk about what is bothering him. Sometimes both processes are warranted and add to one another.

Tell students that they can also ask for a standing ovation when they feel like they want or need one. They simply have to raise their hand and say "I would like a standing ovation." Then give it to them.

I can only close the gap in broken community by meeting hate with love. If I meet hate with hate, I become depersonalized, because creation is so designed that my personality can only be fulfilled in the context of community. When I love, I restore community.

Martin Luther King Jr.

100 the car wash

A lovely little activity was introduced to one of our college classes by a student. He called it the "Car Wash," and for a very good reason, as you'll see.

The Car Wash consists simply of lining up your class or group in two parallel lines quite close together. Then one student is sent through the wash (between the lines) and everyone touches him or her and says words of praise and affection and encouragement. The pats on the back, hand-shaking, and verbal support produce a sparkling, shiny, happy "car" at the end of the wash!

We usually run one or two people through the car wash each day rather than everybody in one big clean-up. That insures that the responses of the washers are fresh, personalized, and enthusiastic. However, putting everyone through the car wash at the end of an intensive experience is a great way to end a session.

> What a strange machine man is! You fill him with bread, wine, fish, and radishes, and out of him comes sighs, laughter, and dreams.
>
> Nikos Kazantzakis
> *Zorba the Greek*

101 hand massaging

A lovely idea for the primary grades is one we saw reported in *Newsweek* magazine. It described Molly Fontaine of the Cambridgeport Children's Center (Tot Lot) in Cambridge, Massachusetts, as a "compassionate, imaginative teacher."

Molly has her children squeeze cream lotion from a tube onto their hands, then rub it gently into the hands of children next to them. This strikes us as a wonderful lesson in sharing and empathy.

This exercise is the kind we like best because it involves action, touch, and extending oneself for another. Back and shoulder rubs also fall into this category.

Try it—the children love it!

Life begets life.
Energy creates energy.
It is by spending oneself
That one becomes rich.

Sarah Bernhardt

For Men only.*
THE KEY TO HEALTH, WEALTH, AND LONGEVITY
Dr. Joyce Brothers

How would you like to be healthier, live longer, and earn more? Without having to go on a diet, do exercises, or work harder (or longer)? Sounds like a never-never idea, doesn't it? Well, there's a very simple prescription that will help you achieve these goals. It was worked out by a group of German psychologists, physicians, and insurance companies who cooperated on a research project designed to find out the secret of long life and success. They found, according to Dr. Arthur Szabo of West Germany, that the key to longer, happier, healthier, wealthier lives for men lies in one single act. All you have to do is:

KISS YOUR WIFE EACH MORNING WHEN YOU LEAVE FOR WORK!

You don't have to *feel* like kissing her; just do it. That's the secret of success.

The meticulous German researchers discovered that men who kiss their wives every morning have fewer automobile accidents on their way to work then men who omit the morning kiss. The good-morning kissers miss less work because of sickness than the non-kissers. And they earn from 20 to 30 percent more money and live some five years longer than men who are stingy with their kisses.

Dr. Szabo explains, "A husband who kisses his wife every morning begins the day with a positive attitude."

Is there any hope for those gentlemen who neglect to deliver that morning kiss? They have a lot going against them, insists Dr. Szabo. These unaffectionate fellows start the day with negative feelings and doubts about their own worth. You see, a kiss is a kind of seal of approval.

If *you* have been rushing out of the house in the morning without kissing your wife, consider changing your ways. It might make a change in your wife, too. Why not try it?

* *Editor's note:* With all the changes in sex roles that are taking place, we imagine that this approach would prove equally effective for a woman kissing her husband before she leaves for work.

102 say hello to EVLN

Here is an excellent model to use with older students or groups. It considers how they respond to relationships that go awry. This two-dimensional model can be applied to dating relationships, friendships, family and marital relationships, and even job-related entanglements.

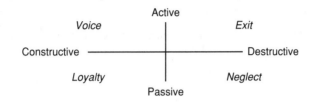

The *active/passive* and *constructive/destructive* poles cross to form four quadrants; four distinct classes of responses to a deteriorating relationship. These four ways of responding are:

1. *Exit (active/destructive)*: End or threaten to end the relationship (i.e., actions that seek to maintain self-esteem, possibly at the expense of the relationship).

2. *Voice (active/constructive)*: Express one's dissatisfaction, with the intent of improving conditions (i.e., actions that seek to maintain both self-esteem and the relationship).

3. *Loyalty (passive/constructive)*: Wait and hope that conditions will improve (i.e., attempt to maintain the relationship, possibly at the expense of self-esteem).

4. *Neglect (passive/destructive)*: Allow but do not actually cause the relationship to atrophy (i.e., actions that are not directed toward maintaining either self-esteem or the relationship).

Following are some typical ways a person would behave who generally selected a particular style of dealing with a failing relationship:

EXIT

I would end the relationship.

I would tell the person that I couldn't take it anymore and our relationship was over.

I would tell my friend that he was not worth the trouble and heartache and that I didn't want to continue the relationship.

I would tell the person that I'd had enough and did not want to put up any more with her selfishness, and then leave.

VOICE

We would talk about why things had come to this point, what we needed to do to make things better, then proceed from there.

I would sit down and talk things out with the other person.

I would ask my friend what was wrong with our relationship.

I would confront my friend with my feelings.

LOYALTY

I would feel that I had invested too much of myself in this relationship to break it off, and hope that we could resume it.

I would like/love my friend enough that I would try to overlook what he had done.

What would be important to me would be how I feel, not what others feel or say about my friend, so I would stick by her.

I would try to ignore what my friend was doing and see how foolish it was and would resume our relationship.

NEGLECT

I would feel that it really didn't matter if our relationship ended or got worse.

I would emotionally withdraw to avoid getting hurt any more.

I would probably just kind of quit; I wouldn't try to salvage the relationship.

I would back off and let the relationship drift.

Begin your session with the students by asking them how people typically respond when they're in a failing relationship and record their answers on the chalk board. They will likely come up with ideas similar to those above.

When this has run its course, ask them to write down in their journals or on paper those ways from the list that *they* have recently used to deal with a relationship that is going or has gone sour.

Now, tell them about the EVLN model while putting it on the board beside their earlier responses or on a separate chart. Then, with the group, go over each of the responses and label them E, V, L, N as appropriate.

Have group members privately examine the responses each has recently used and, after drawing the two-dimensional model on paper, have them put an "*x*" in the appropriate quadrant for *each of their responses.*

Then have a general discussion asking such questions as:

Do you notice a pattern in your own responses?

Did you learn anything about yourself?

What did you learn or get fresh perspective on?

Can you use this model to change the way you respond?

How hard is it going to be to change?

What is required?

This lesson can be useful and even very important to people for their whole lives. As long as we live, we're in relationships that wax and wane, and we need to learn productive ways to make them work.

We suggest that you make a handout of the EVLN model and the definitions or examples of each category as we've shown above and urge your students to keep them. They're bound to need them at some time in their lives!

This exercise was adapted from the work of C. E. Rusbult as it appeared in *Intimate Relationships,* edited by D. Perlman and S. Duck (Newbury Park, CA: Sage Publications, 1990), pp. 209–234.

The building blocks of self-esteem are skills. The more skillful a person, the more likely that he or she will be able to cope in life situations. By fostering skills of personal and social responsibility, schools can help students increase their behavioral options. Having a number of behavioral options makes it easier to make ethical choices and develop skills to function effectively.

Toward a State of Esteem.
The final report of the California Task Force to Promote Self-Esteem and Personal and Social Responsibility.

103 making your wants known

Implicit in every question, statement of resentment, hostile comment, etc., is a demand of a "want" on the speaker's part. For example, if a student reacts to a statement of another pupil by saying something like, "Oh, that's stupid!" he really is trying to communicate, "I want . . ." or "I demand . . ." His want or demand is veiled by his hostile remark; consequently, listeners can't be sure exactly what it is that he wants. How much clearer it would be if he simply stated instead, "I want to be heard on this issue," or "I demand that we vote," or whatever it is he really wants.

Some teachers will cringe at the thought of encouraging students to state their demands. Our experience, however, leads us to believe that after the initial shock to teachers and students and some experimenting with the concept, a class will settle down to a very reasonable use of this communication tool—and many wants and demands are met simply because they are clearly known to the listeners.

Begin the exercise by asking the students:

> *What would make this class better for you? If you could make the people in this group do something to make the class better for you, what would you demand we do? Begin your want with: "I want this class to . . ."*

This exercise helps pupils realize that they do have a right to make demands, just as those people have a right to refuse meeting those demands. At a later stage you may want to expand the exercise to include making demands or wants on the teacher—this usually proves to be a good feedback mechanism—and on specific students in the class. When making demands, children should face the person, say his name, and then make his want known. For instance, "Gerald, I want you to stop pulling my hair during recess," or "Martha, I want you to make less noise when I am trying to read." Some typical responses that have been generated by this exercise are:

> I demand that Nina and Lucy quit bugging me about things I bring to school.

> I want the members of this class to listen to me when I am talking.

eight

in closing—

As we said in the beginning, this is *a practical book.* That was no doubt why the first edition was so enormously successful, which, in turn, has inspired us to stay up to date and to create new activities to enhance self-esteem.

There is great satisfaction in working on behalf of teachers and young people. We have a sense of doing our share to create a better world, as every good professor, teacher, and counselor must surely feel.

This is an era that emphasizes achievement, academic competence, and peak performance. That's good. The success of teachers and principals in inner-city and other schools where they've thrown down the gauntlet and insisted on high standards of performance and conduct is testimony to the desire and capability of most learners to achieve academically, no matter what social or environmental handicaps are put in their way.

There is nothing in this book that will do anything but *increase* the likelihood of scholastic success.

We join hands with all of you in hoping and praying for—and striving to foster—sane, happy, knowledgeable, capable people who can have the chance to live in a safe and peaceful world.

Jack Canfield
Harold Clive Wells

annotated bibliography of the best available resources

If you have come this far in the book, you are ready to go further in your quest to develop positive self-concepts and high self-esteem in your students. Fortunately, there are a lot of very good resources available to interested educators, counselors, facilitators, and parents. There are many more resources than we could possibly list here, so we have listed those resources that have been the most valuable to us in our work with students of all ages in all kinds of circumstances.

If you would like a more complete listing of resources, write to Self-Esteem Seminars, 6035 Bristol Parkway, Culver City, CA 90230, and request a copy of **The Self-Esteem Store Catalogue.** The catalogue lists over 350 products—books, curriculum guides, workbooks, cassette tapes, videotapes, and other self-esteem resources, representing 135 publishers. Each entry is annotated along with a full-color picture of the cover of each resource.

The Self-Esteem Shop, 422 N. Telegraph, Dearborn, MI 48128 (Phone: 313-549-0511; fax 313-561-8741), also has a mail order catalogue listing over 1,000 titles in self-esteem, family issues, communication skills, alcohol and drug prevention, sexual abuse, adolescent issues, children's books, women's issues, personal growth, neuro-linguistic programming, and counseling skills. The catalogue only lists titles and is not annotated, but it is an incredibly complete collection of available resources. You can order by phone, fax, or mail.

Three publishers that also have a heavy emphasis on self-esteem education are the following:

B. L. Winch & Associates/Jalmar Press, Skypark Business Center, 2675 Skypark Drive, Suite 204, Torrance, CA 90505 (Phone:800-662-9662), is one of the major publishers of materials in the fields of self-esteem and affective education. Write or call for a free catalogue.

Health Communications, 3201 S.W. 15th Street, Deerfield Beach, FL 33442-8190 (Phone: 800-851-9100). Their books and tape focus on building self-esteem, healing the inner child, recovery from addictions, and dysfunctional families. Write or phone for a catalogue.

Zephyr Press, 430 S. Essex Lane, Tucson, AZ 85711, is another publisher that carries many books and curricula in this field. Write for a free catalogue.

Three other catalogues that make finding books on self-esteem easy are as follows:

ETR Associates, P.O. Box 1830, Santa Cruz, CA 95061-1830 (Phone: 800-321-4407), is a nonprofit organization dedicated to developing and distributing quality materials in the field of health education, family life, sexuality, communication, and self-esteem.

Kidsrights, 10100 Park Cedar Drive, Charlotte, NC 28210 (Phone: 800-892-KIDS), is a comprehensive source of prevention and education materials from preschool to professional training. Includes parenting, counseling, self-esteem, stress management, child abuse prevention, teen suicide, drugs and alcohol, and teen pregnancy prevention.

Paperbacks for Educators, 1240 Ridge Road, Ballwin, MO 63021 (Phone: 800-227-2591), is yet another valuable catalogue containing hundreds of books and curricula on all aspects of teaching with a strong emphasis on building self-esteem and dealing with the affective dimensions of education. Write for a free catalogue. They have both a teacher's and a school counselor's edition of their catalogue.

1. Books that we feel are special and important:

Awareness by John Stevens (New York: Bantam Books, 1973). This is an excellent book combining theory and over 100 exercises drawn from gestalt awareness training, almost all of which can be used in the classroom. The exercises include personal awareness; communication with others; guided visualizations; exercises for pairs and for groups of students; exercises utilizing art, movement, and sound; and a special section entitled "To the Group Leader or Teacher." We highly recommend this book.

Schools without Failure by William Glasser (New York: Harper & Row, 1969). Glasser offers a powerful and effective approach to reduce school failures—an approach based on personal involvement, relevance, and thinking. Through the use of the "classroom meeting," he demonstrates how to reach negatively oriented, failure-conscious students and how to help them aim for positive goal-setting, personal achievement, and individual responsibility.

Self-Concept and School Achievement by William W. Purkey (Englewood Cliffs, NJ: Prentice-Hall, 1970). In this classic, Purkey explores the growing emphasis on the student's subjective and personal self-evaluation as a dominant influence on his or her success in school. He explains how the self-concept develops in social interaction and what happens to it in school. He also suggests ways for the teacher to reinforce positive and realistic self-concepts in students.

Inviting School Success: A Self-Concept Approach to Teaching and Learning by William W. Purkey and John M. Novak (Belmont, CA: Wadsworth, 1984). This important book approaches self-concept development from both a philosophical and a practical basis. It provides a solid framework for student–teacher interactions that invite rather than disinvite the student to participate in the learning process. The book contains 225 specific suggestions for teachers, counselors, school bus drivers, school secretaries, and school administrators. Lots of valuable ideas here!

The Antecedents of Self-Esteem by Stanley Coopersmith (San Francisco: W. H. Freeman, 1967). This is a doctoral dissertation on the self-esteem of a group of junior high school boys. It is academic reading but has come to be considered a classic for anyone seriously interested in the development of self-esteem in educational settings.

Healing the Shame That Binds You by John Bradshaw (Deerfield Beach FL: Health Communications, 1988). Bradshaw shows how toxic shame is the core problem in our compulsions, codependencies, addictions, and the drive to superachieve. Offers affirmations, visualizations, and other ways to help relieve the shame that binds us. A truly profound book on the problem of low self-esteem and how to raise it. Also available on audio tape.

The Four Conditions of Self-Esteem by Reynold Bean. Available from ETR Associates, P.O. Box 1830, Santa Cruz, CA 95061-1830 (Phone: 800-321-4407). According to Bean's model, children attain strong self-esteem when they experience positive feelings within four conditions: Connectiveness, Uniqueness, Power, and Models. This book provides a comprehensive blueprint for increasing these conditions in individual students, in the classroom, and throughout the school.

Beyond Self-Esteem: Developing a Genuine Sense of Human Value by Nancy Curry and Carl Johnson. Available from the National Association for the Education of Young Children, 1834 Connecticut Avenue, N.W., Washington, DC 20009-5786. This book is one of the best for anyone dealing with preschool-age children. Parents, teachers, administrators, and policymakers can go beyond naive conceptions of self-esteem as an isolated entity and toward an understanding of self-esteem as a dynamic, multidimensional phenomenon that must be viewed in larger context of children's social, cognitive, moral, and personality development. Highly recommended.

IALAC: I Am Lovable and Capable, A Modern Allegory on the Classical Put-Down by Sidney Simon, Ph.D. (Niles, IL: Argus, 1977). Putdowns and personal digs do more damage than most of us imagine. The IALAC Story beautifully deals with this problem for children and adults alike. This little story has become a classic in its own right.

Student Self-Esteem, A Vital Element of School Success edited by Gary Walz and Jeanne Bleuer (P.O. Box 1403, Ann Arbor, MI 48106: Counseling and Personnel Services, 1992). An exceptionally comprehensive and useful resource on K–12 student self-esteem and staff development for teachers and counselors. Over 60 articles by outstanding authorities offering practical and field-validated programs and ideas.

Toward a State of Esteem: The Final Report of the California Task Force to Promote Self-Esteem and Personal and Social Responsibility (Sacramento: State of California, 1990). This historic document is one that you should have in your library. It will be helpful to you in convincing administrators, school board members, and parents of the value of self-esteem building in education. It is the final report of a state task force that met for three years in California to determine how best to raise the self-esteem of California citizens so as to lower the school dropout rate, teen pregnancy rate, crime rate, and incidences of child and spouse abuse and drug and alcohol abuse. The task force report contains much valuable information and, unlike many government reports, is easy to read, is full of inspirational quotes, and contains an annotated list of resources. Send a check for $4.00 to Bureau of Publications, California State Department of Education, P.O. Box 271, Sacramento, CA 95802-0271.

Appendixes to: Toward a State of Esteem, The California Task Force to Promote Self-Esteem. A listing of self-esteem resources, research, programs, books, videos, and projects. Available from the address above for $4.00.

Revolution from Within: A Book of Self-Esteem by Gloria Steinem (Boston: Little, Brown, 1992). This book should be read by everyone in the United States. It has so much valuable information about self-esteem in general and girls' and women's self-esteem in particular. If you are a woman, are married to one, or teach girls, please read this book. It will give you new insights and understandings about how self-esteem is formed and how to build it purposefully in yourself and others.

How to Raise Your Self-Esteem by Nathaniel Branden (New York: Bantam, 1987). This is a practical guide to how to raise your self-confidence, self-respect, and self-esteem.

2. Books that contain valuable activities for enhancing self-concept and building self-esteem:

Self-Esteem in the Classroom: A Curriculum Guide by Jack Canfield and others, (Culver City, CA: Self-Esteem Seminars, 1986). This book is really the first sequel to the book you hold in your hands. It contains the best of ten years' of research into new methods and techniques to build self-esteem. It is currently being used by over 8,000 teachers in all 50 states and in 15 countries. It contains over 200 activities for all grade levels—149 of which can be used at any grade level from kindergarten through high school, and an additional 75 activities specifically for elementary use. Its eight sections include "Building an Environment of Positive Support," "The Power of Our Thoughts," "The Power of Imagination," "The Power of Acknowledgment," "Accepting My Body," "Self-Awareness," "Learning to Handle My Feelings," and "The Elementary Curriculum." There are over 379 pages of powerful, yet easy-to-use activities that are not in either *100 Ways* or *101 Ways*. Write or call 800-2-ESTEEM for a free brochure.

101 Ways to Develop Student Self-Esteem and Responsibility (Volumes 1 and 2) by Jack Canfield and Frank Siccone (Boston: Allyn & Bacon, 1993). These two volumes contain what is really the third book in a series of self-esteem building activities, with a strong focus on building personal and social responsibility. There are 101 activities designed to build self-esteem and teach responsibility to junior high, high school, and adult learners. The activities are divided into the following sections: "The Teacher as Leader," "Teacher as Role Model," "Empowerment," "Teaching as a Loving Activity," "Teaching as Transformation," "Secrets of Happiness and Success," "Social Responsibility," and the "Community as Classroom." *101 Ways* is a natural progression from the book you are reading. We highly recommend it.

Esteem Builders: A K–8 Self-Esteem Curriculum for Improving Student Achievement, Behavior and School Climate by Michele Borba (Rolling Hills Estate, CA: Jalmar Press, 1989). This is probably the most valuable self-esteem resource published in the past ten years for elementary and middle school teachers. It contains over 250 activities, a self-esteem assessment chart, a forty-week activity lesson planner, lots of reproducible worksheets, and schoolwide self-esteem activities as well as individual classroom activities. It is based on strategies that have been field-tested for over six years in over 60,000 classrooms. There is also an extensive annotated list of children's books dealing with self-esteem issues. This is a must for elementary and middle school teachers.

Self-Esteem: A Classroom Affair—101 Ways to Help Children to Like Themselves (Volumes 1 and 2) by Michele Borba and Craig Borba (San Francisco: Harper San Francisco, 1978). These two volumes contain hundreds of other wonderful, easy-to-use esteem-building exercises for elementary school children. Though not as extensive a resource as the Borba book listed above, it contains many wonderful additional activities.

Project Self-Esteem by Sandy McDaniel and Peggy Bielen. Available from B. L. Winch & Associates/Jalmar Press, Skypark Business Center, 2675 Skypark Drive, Suite 204, Torrance, CA 90505 (Phone: 800-662-9662). This is a truly delightful K–8 program that can be conducted by the teacher or by parent volunteers in the school. It is practical, inexpensive, and effective. Used by over 2,000 schools with more than 400,000 participants, the program has undergone extensive field testing and revisions. It will greatly improve school climate as well as student self-esteem. There is also training available.

The Best Self-Esteem Activities—For the Elementary Grades by Terri Akin, David Cowan, Gerry Dunne, Susanna Palomares, Dianne Schilling, and Sandy Schuster. Available from Innerchoice Publishing, P.O. Box 2476, Spring Valley, CA 91979 (Phone: 619-698-2437). This workbook is a collection of the most effective instructional strategies available for helping students. The exercises directly enhance the self-esteem of students by engaging them in experiences that develop a wide range of life and academic skills and, in the process, build confidence and a strong sense of personal and social responsibility.

Unlocking Doors to Self-Esteem: Content-Oriented Activities for Grades 7–12 by Lynn Fox (Rolling Hills Estates, CA: Jalmar Press, 1990). Contains curriculum content objectives with underlying social objectives in English, Drama, Social Science, Career Education, Science, etc. There are over 100 lesson plans on self-esteem activities that are easily infused into secondary academic curriculum.

Enhancing Self-Esteem by Diane Frey and C. Jesse Carlock (3400 Kilgore Avenue, Muncie, IN 47304: Accelerated Development, 1984). This is a unique book in that it combines in-depth theory with practical activities better than almost any other book. The activities are appropriate for teens and adults.

Spinning Inward—Using Guided Imagery with Children for Learning, Creativity and Relaxation by Maureen Murdock (Boston: Shambhala Publications, 1987). Maureen is an educator, therapist, and artist who discovered the benefits of guided imagery with her own children and then took these techniques into her classroom.

"He Hit Me Back First!" Creative Visualization Activities for Parenting and Teaching by Eva D. Fugitt. Available from Jalmar Press, 2675 Skypark Drive, Suite 204, Torrance, CA 90505 (Phone: 310-784-0016). This workbook presents activities for home and school that will help youngsters become aware of choice and of their own inner authority. Parents and teachers will love the simple techniques for guiding children toward self-correcting behavior based on knowledge of their "Wise Part Within." Her methods show the child that he can discipline himself, that he has a choice, and that, with choice, there are responses that enhance or lower self-esteem.

The Centering Book by Gay Hendricks and Russell Wills (Englewood Cliffs, NJ: Prentice Hall, 1975). This book contains numerous awareness activities for students, parents, and teachers. The focus is on how to become more centered and more relaxed.

The Second Centering Book by Gay Hendricks and Thomas B. Roberts (Englewood Cliffs, NJ: Prentice-Hall, 1978). This book goes further than the first book, with a much broader focus. It contains numerous activities to help teachers and students develop their intuition, work with guided fantasy, enhance communication skills, energize themselves, and center themselves. You will find lots of good activities here.

3. Self-esteem curriculum guides that we like a lot:

Building Self-Esteem: Elementary Edition by Robert Reasoner (Palo Alto, CA: Consulting Psychologists Press, 1982). This is a very solid curriculum guide with plenty of reproducible worksheets for students at the elementary and middle school levels. This is one of the best programs around. Reasoner divides the curriculum into five basic esteem building blocks: security, identity, purpose, belonging, and competence. The *Teacher's Manual* contains 125 worksheets and 500 suggestions for teachers. The *Administrator's Manual* provides staff development material and suggestions for developing teacher self-esteem. A *Parent Guide* is also available to support the program.

Building Self-Esteem: Secondary Edition by Robert Reasoner and Gail Dusa (Palo Alto, CA: Consulting Psychologists Press, 1992). Working on the same five areas described in the resource for elementary students, this curriculum uses reproducible worksheets broken down by grade level. Gail has also provided an activities calendar, a cross-reference section for children with special needs, and a teacher's manual.

Building Self-Esteem with Koala-Roo Can-Do (K–3) by Laura Fendel. Available from The Self-Esteem Store, 3201 S.W. 15th Street, Deerfield Beach, FL 33442–8190. With Koala-Roo Can-Do as the class mascot, you can make a real difference in the way your students feel about themselves and the way they approach learning. Includes daily record sheets, bulletin board visuals, buttons, awards, games, puppets, and much more.

Esteem Builders: The Complete Program by Dr. Michele Borba. Available from B. L. Winch & Associates/Jalmar Press, Skypark Business Center, 2675 Skypark Drive, Suite 204, Torrance, CA 90505 (Phone 800-662-9662). At last, a totally cross-correlated self-esteem curriculum that allows school boards, district administrators, school administrators, teachers, parents, and students all to experience the growth of positive self-esteem with various components in the same program! This program has an upbeat video showing what successful self-esteem programs look like at school sites; a trainer of trainers manual, a video, and six audio cassettes to help each school or district train its own people on how to use all the components; a staff development manual to grow self-esteem in the personnel at each individual site; a *Home Esteem Builder Manual* with activities that support parent involvement in raising the self-esteem of their children (and their own in the process); an *Esteem Builders Teacher's Manual* full of over 250 activities woven in, around, and through the five building blocks of self-esteem and cross-correlated to both grade level and curriculum content; posters for the classroom; a Sparky puppet with 30 scripted activity cards; an overview that shows how the components interrelate; and a complete resource guide listing self-esteem resources, formal and informal assessments, research and statistics, plus an index cross-referencing the over 1,000 esteem-building activities in the complete program by esteem component and targeted audience. WOW!

GOAL: *Guidance Opportunities for Affective Learning,* Irvine Unified School District, Guidance Projects, 31-B West Yale Loop, Irvine, CA 92714. Created as a Title IV-C project for grades K–6 to teach self-control, responsibility, and ways to interact with others.

The GOALS Program by Jack Canfield and Larry Price. Available from Foundation for Self-Esteem, 6035 Bristol Parkway, Culver City, CA 90230 (Phone: 310-568-1505). This is a multicultural, multimedia motivational and self-esteem development program designed for at-risk adults. It contains three and a half hours of video, an 80-page workbook, a one-hour audio cassette, and a comprehensive facilitator's manual. The program has been used successfully in numerous community colleges, adult education programs, 38 county welfare programs, homeless shelters, San Quentin, and the Maryland state prisons. Write for a brochure.

Horizons 2000 by Dr. Cheryl G. Bartholomew. Distributed by B. L. Winch & Associates/Jalmar Press, Skypark Business Center, 2675 Skypark Drive, Suite 204, Torrance, CA 90505 (Phone: 800-662-9662). This is "A Career and Life Planning Curriculum for Girls in Grades 5–12" developed as a direct response to the 1992 American Association of University Women study that showed girls' self-esteem decreases faster between ages 7 and 15 than that of boys. As a result, girls often opt out of math and science courses. This new program provides role models and activities that encourage girls to look more seriously at these subjects. The program includes teacher, parent, and student manuals as well as video and audio cassettes. Call B. L. Winch for a complete brochure.

Here's Looking at You 2000, Comprehensive Health Education Foundations, 29832 Pacific Highway South, Seattle, WA 98198. This is a very comprehensive drug education curriculum that includes extensive information about the negative effects of drugs as well as numerous lessons on building self-esteem and other affective dimensions of the students. The program is expensive, but it includes books, audio cassettes, computer software, puppets, pamphlets, and video cassettes. Write for a free catalogue.

How to Be Successful in Less Than 10 Minutes per Day by Robert Paull. Thomas Jefferson Research Center, 1143 North Lake Avenue, Pasadena, CA 91104. This program is intended to support a schoolwide effort to improve climate, attendance, achievement, and self-discipline. The program includes 180 daily lessons.

I CAN by Zig Ziglar. Positive Life Attitudes for America, 13642 Omega, Dallas, TX 75234. Based on the positive mental attitude seminars of motivational speaker Zig Ziglar, this program contains lesson plans, school ideas, posters, and buttons. Separate materials are available for grades K–4, grades 5–8, and high school. Each course is designed to cover 80 hours.

Innerchange by Uvaldo Palomares and Geraldine Ball. Innerchoice, 9602 Montemas Drive, Spring Valley, CA 91977. Aimed at grades 7–12, this curriculum uses the magic circle discussion approach to deal with feelings, relationships, problem solving, goal setting, and several other related areas.

More Teachable Moments by Cliff Durfee. Live, Love, Laugh, P.O. Box 9432, San Diego, CA 92169 (Phone: 619-270-0252). This program, which is similar to the magic circle program in many ways, develops communication skills, self-esteem, and positive mental health through encouraging listening, sharing of feelings, guided imagery, and goal setting. The materials are built around ten lessons, each lesson taking several class sessions.

Mother-Daughter Choices. Advocacy Press, P.O. Box 236, Santa Barbara, CA 93012. (Phone: 805-962-2728). This program brings mothers and their pre-teen daughters together for six two-hour sessions for the purpose of motivating the girls to expand their vision of themselves and their capabilities, improve their self-esteem and their self-confidence, and teach them valuable life skills such as problem solving, decision making, goal setting, and assertive, responsible behavior. A handbook and a two-hour video are available.

Music Is a Gift of Love, A Self-Esteem Character Development Program (Grades K–5) by Carol Eberle. Available from Carol Eberle, 2837 Lomitas Avenue, Santa Rosa, CA 95404 (Phone: 707-579-2510). A curriculum guide accompanied by a songbook and lyrics for the kids to sing along with. The music tape does the teaching! The tape contains 26 delightful songs reinforcing good self-image and encouraging positive attitudes. It is especially helpful to teachers with little or no music background.

Personality Fitness Training by John Hart and Richard Revheim. Available from the Institute for the Study of Personal Intelligence, 11850 Wilshire Boulevard, Suite 201, Los Angeles, CA 90025, published 1986. Aimed at grades 3–12, this curriculum is designed to enhance personality and build self-esteem through a series of exercises to develop personal intelligence, self-esteem, and stress resilience.

POPS, Power of Positive Students. International Foundation, 4325 Dick Pond Road, Myrtle Beach, SC 29575 (Phone: 800-521-2741). POPS International Foundation is a nonprofit educational foundation begun under the leadership of Dr. William Mitchell. The major functions of the foundation are to acquaint interested individuals with details of the program's structure and execution; to create and make available materials that assist in the understanding and implementation of the program; to provide workshops and seminars and to serve as a clearinghouse for compiling and disseminating data about self-esteem and related areas of concern; and to share successful activities, strategies, and ideas with educators all across the world. Write or call for their quarterly catalogue.

POPS Multi Media Program (Power of Positive Students). Positive Communications, Inc., 70 Route 22, Pawling, NY 12564 (Phone: 914-855-9600). This is a multimedia video and audio self-esteem program for elementary school students. It was field-tested in all elementary schools in the state of West Virginia during the 1988–89 school year and received very positive reviews. Write or call for more information.

Positive Action Self-Concept Curriculum by Carol Allred. Positive Action, P.O. Box 2347, Twin Falls, ID 83301-7440. This comprehensive self-esteem program includes separate materials and worksheets for each grade level from kindergarten through grade 7. The curriculum is designed to take 15–20 minutes per day throughout the year.

PLUS: Promoting Learning and Understanding Self. Irvine Unified School District, Guidance Projects Office, 31-B West Yale Loop, Irvine, CA 92714. Aimed at grades 9–12, this curriculum is designed to improve academic achievement, behavior, and self-concept of students having academic and social problems, though it could be used with any class. It contains 82 lessons in problem solving, stress management, and social skills.

Project Self-Esteem by Sandy McDaniel and Peggy Bielen. B. L. Winch & Associates/Jalmar Press, Skypark Business Center, 2675 Skypark Drive, Suite 204, Torrance, CA 90505 (Phone:

800-662-9662). Aimed at grades 2–6, this curriculum is designed to develop self-esteem through awareness of feelings, uniqueness, goal setting, friendships, and development of skills in listening, communication, and social interaction. The sessions are activity-oriented. Training is also available from the authors, who can be contacted at Project Self-Esteem, P.O. Box 16001, Newport Beach, CA 92659 (Phone: 800-756-7856).

Pumsy in Pursuit of Excellence, An 8-Week Cognitive Self-Esteem Program by Jill Anderson (Grades K–3). Timberline Press, P.O. Box 70071, Eugene, OR 97401 (Phone: 503-345-1771). Skills are introduced in a nonthreatening way through a lovable dragon named Pumsy. Helps kids learn to shift self-esteem from being externally based to internally based. Develops long-term approaches to problem solving, making responsible choices, improving social skills, and overcoming negative thought patterns. Includes a leader's guide, 10 color posters, 9 parent letters, 420 stickers, 7 transparencies, color storybook, puppet, songbook, 35 activity sheets, and a song cassette tape.

QUEST: Skills for Adolescence. Quest International, 537 Jones Road, Granville, OH 43023-0566 (Phone: 800-446-2700, fax: 614-522-6580). Aimed at grades 7–12, this curriculum focuses on parenting, family relationships, dating and marriage, money and budgeting, self-esteem, self-discipline, responsibility, and other important life skills. They have also have developed an elementary school program entitled *Skills for Growing.* Both programs are widely used in over 20,000 schools all across the United States and Canada, as well as in 30 other countries. The Skills for Adolescence Program is available in six languages, including Spanish and French. Requires three days of training before you can teach the program. Your local Lions Club will often underwrite the cost of training and materials. Contact Quest International for more information.

Self-Esteem (middle school and junior high) and *Personal and Social Responsibility* (high school) by Connie Dembrowsky. Institute for Affective Skill Development, P.O. Box 880, La Luz, NM 88337 (Phone: 505-437-5282). Two comprehensive semester-long self-esteem and responsibility curriculums for junior and senior high school students. Materials include a Teacher's Guide, Student Workbooks, and a Parent Guide. Each curriculum contains 85 lessons. Especially effective with at-risk students. Highly recommended.

Self-Science: The Subject is Me by Karen Stone. Nueva Day Center, 6565 Skyline Boulevard, Hillsborough, CA 94010 (Phone: 415-348-2272). This self-science curriculum is based on the outstanding work of Professor Gerald Weinstein at the University of Massachusetts. It is designed to equip students with the necessary affective and cognitive skills to study themselves within small group laboratory situations. The program is designed to build self-understanding. It includes 64 lessons.

Smile, You're Worth It by Margo Kluth and Dorothy McCarthy. Me and My Inner Self, Inc., P.O. Box 1396, La Canada–Flintridge, CA 91011. Aimed at grades 7–12, this program is designed to lead young people to the discovery of self-worth. It contains specific exercises and activities to students remove concepts that limit their potential.

STAGES: Education for Families in Transition. Irvine Unified School District, Guidance Projects Office, 31-B West Yale Loop, Irvine CA 92714. Aimed at grades K–8, this curriculum addresses problems children experience with divorce and family changes. It includes workbooks, tapes, task cards, and handbooks for parents and teachers. STAGES II, for grades 7–12, is also available.

STAR: Social Thinking and Reasoning. Irvine Unified School District, Guidance Projects Office, 31-B west Yale Loop, Irvine, CA 92714. Aimed at grades 6–8, this curriculum is designed to teach critical social skills, self-concept, and drug abuse prevention. It contains 50 lessons, with handbooks and cassette tapes.

The Dynamics of Relationships by Pat Kramer. Equal Partners/The Self-Esteem Institute, 3371 Beaverwood Lane, Silver Spring, MD 20906 (Phone: 301-871-9665, fax: 301-871-9667). This life skills curriculum can be run as a five-day a week, year-long course, or used to supplement any ongoing substance abuse prevention, teen pregnancy prevention, or youth-at-risk program. There are student manuals and teachers' manuals available for both the teen/young adult age and the preteen (grades 4–7) levels. Training is available but not required.

The Human Development Program (also known as *The Magic Circle Program*) by Harold Bessel and Uvaldo Palomares. Palomares and Associates, P.O. Box 1577, Spring Valley, CA 92077 (Phone: 619-670-6654). This is another widely used, easy-to-conduct program that develops self-esteem and mental health by teaching communication skills, self-awareness, self-acceptance, and self-expression by encouraging students to regularly share their thoughts and feelings in a small group setting.

Thinking, Changing, Rearranging: Improving Self-Esteem in Young People by Jill Anderson. Timberline Press, P.O. Box 70187, Eugene, OR 97401 (Phone: 503-484-6194). This illustrated text/manual/workbook is based on rational-emotive therapy and neurolinguistic programming (NLP). It shows young people how to gain better control of how they feel about themselves and the world.

Tribes by Jeanne Gibbs. Center for Human Development, 3702 Mount Diablo Boulevard, Lafayette, CA 94549 (Phone: 415-937-1075). This is a widely used program designed to enhance communication skills and interrelationships between students and their peers and students and adults. The program is appropriate for elementary, junior high, and high school students. Extensive training is available but is not required.

Values in Action by Gene Bedley. People Wise Publications, 14252 East Mall, Irvine, CA 92714, Published in 1993. This is a comprehensive program for schools to promote values. Regardless of the problems children face, without a program that equips kids with tools and language, inappropriate behavior persists. When kids know what their values are they can make decisions! The *Values in Action* program includes: posters, affirmations, value ventures themes, integrity creed, respect report, and numerous activities to promote respect, integrity, compassion, positive mental attitude, perseverance, cooperation and initiative.

4. Discipline from a self-esteem perspective:

Cooperative Discipline—A Teacher's Guide: How to Manage Your Classroom and Promote Self-Esteem by Linda Albert. Available from American Guidance Service, P.O. Box 99, Circle Pines, MN 55014-1796 (Phone: 800-328-2560). This is one of the most self-esteem oriented approaches to discipline you will ever find. It is a total classroom approach that teaches you how to intervene quickly and effectively at the moment of misbehavior, to encourage students over the long haul to build self-esteem by insisting they take responsibility for their behavior, and ultimately to gain even the toughest kid's cooperation.

Discipline with Purpose: A Developmental Approach to Teaching Self-Discipline by Barbara Vasiloff and Paula Lenz, 1315 S. 124th Street, Omaha, NE 68144 (Phone: 402-691-0799). *Discipline with Purpose* is a developmental approach to teaching self-discipline covering grades K–12. The program empowers children to become self-directed through the development of fifteen self-discipline skills. Both materials and live trainings are available.

How to Discipline Children without Feeling Guilty by Harris Clemes and Reynold Bean (Los Angeles: Price Stern Sloan, 1978, 1990). Lots of practical advice from two self-esteem experts.

How to Teach Children Responsibility by Harris Clemes and Reynold Bean (Los Angeles: Price Stern Sloan, 1978, 1990). This practical handbook provides tested methods that will help both parents and teachers pass on to their children a sense of high self-esteem and both personal and social responsibility.

Positive Discipline by Jane Nelsen (New York: Ballantine, 1981, 1987). This is an excellent resource for both home and school. Every adult who works with children of any age should master the concepts and techniques in this book, which covers how to teach children self-discipline, responsibility, cooperation, problem-solving skills, and self-motivation.

Positive Discipline in the Classroom by Jane Nelsen, Lynn Lott and H. Stephen Glenn (Rocklin, CA: Prima Publishing, 1993). Outlines how to conduct successful classroom meetings where students learn to listen, take turns, hear different points of view, negotiate, communicate, and take responsibility for their own behavior as they discuss moral, ethical, and behavioral issues as well as work together to solve classroom problems.

Raising a Responsible Child by Don Dinkmeyer and Gary D. McKay (New York: Simon and Schuster, 1973). This is a valuable basic resource.

Responsibility—The Most Basic R, A Curriculum for Promoting Self-Esteem by Frank Siccone, Ed.D. (San Francisco: The Siccone Institute, 1987). Students learn how to set their own goals, work with the teacher and each other, make commitments, and get the most out of school. Includes handouts, activity suggestions, and discussion questions. Contains 20 units, each about 45 minutes long, designed for use in the classroom.

Teaching Children Self-Discipline . . . at Home and at School: New Ways for Parents and Teachers to Build Self-Control, Self-Esteem, and Self-Reliance by Thomas Gordon (New York: Times Books, 1989). Dr. Gordon makes a provocative case against punitive power-based methods of discipline—which only causes new problems—and advances a very workable alternative. Children learn self-discipline, responsibility, cooperation, and consideration—resulting in greater self-esteem.

21st Century Discipline: Teaching Students Responsibility and Self-Control by Jane Bluestein (Jefferson City, MO: Scholastic Professional Books, 1988). Practical and specific strategies to help create a classroom where the majority of student behavior is on task. Shows you how to elicit responsible, internally motivated cooperation, how to avoid rebellious, hostile behavior, offer choices within limits, and depersonalize conflict.

5. Books on self-esteem for teenagers to read:

You and Self-Esteem: A Book for Young People by Bettie B. Youngs. Available from B. L. Winch & Associates/Jalmar Press, Skypark Business Center, 2675 Skypark Drive, Suite 204, Torrance,

CA 90505 (Phone: 800-662-9662). This comprehensive workbook for young people provides a thorough understanding of self-esteem and offers practical skills to help youth value, protect, and nourish their own sense of self and well-being.

Choices: A Teen Woman's Journal for Self-Awareness and Personal Planning by Mindy Bingham, Judy Edmondson, and Sandy Styker. Advocacy Press, P.O. Box 236, Santa Barbara, CA 93102 (Grades 7–12). This national bestseller is a teen woman's journal for self-awareness and personal planning. It contains thought-provoking exercises that prompt young people to think seriously about their future.

Challenges: A Young Man's Journal for Self-Awareness and Personal Planning by Mindy Bingham, Judy Edmondson, and Sandy Styker. Advocacy Press, P.O. Box 236, Santa Barbara, CA 93102 (grades 7–12). This book is a young man's journal for self-awareness and personal planning. *Challenges* addresses the myths and hard realities that teenage boys often face as they enter adulthood.

There is an instructors' guide available from the publisher for the two books listed above.

Fighting Invisible Tigers: A Stress Management Guide for Teens by Earl Hipp (Minneapolis, MN: Free Spirit Publishing, 1985). Teaches teens how to take control of their lives and assert themselves so that they get their needs met.

Heart Smarts: Teenage Guide for the Puzzle of Life by Doc Lew Childre (P.O. Box 66, Boulder Creek, CA: Planetary Publications, 1991). Is a powerful hands-on manual written in a fun, user-friendly style for teenagers, their parents and teachers. Contains keys to managing stress, building heart-power and self-esteem, managing their mental and emotional energies and improving their relationships.

Secrets of Life Every Teen Needs to Know by Terry and Sean Paulson (San Juan Capistrano, CA: Joy Publishing, 1990). Teaches kids how to learn from successful people without giving up their own uniqueness. A teenager's "Life 101."

Stick Up for Yourself!: Every Kid's Guide to Personal Power and Positive Self-Esteem by Gershon Kaufman and Lev Raphael (Minneapolis, MN: Free Spirit Publishing, 1990). Teaches kids to understand their true feelings, dreams, and needs and how to stick up for themselves at school, at home, and on the playground.

Teen-Esteem: A Self-Direction Manual for Young Adults by Pat Palmer and Melissa Alberti Froehner (San Luis Obispo, CA: Impact Publishers, 1989). This is a book for teens to read that will help them feel good about being themselves. It helps them to build the skills they will need to handle peer pressure, substance abuse, sexual expression, and the many other challenges of adolescence.

The Creative Journal for Teens: Making Friends with Yourself by Lucia Capacchione (North Hollywood, CA: Newcastle, 1992). Offers easy techniques for journal writing that enable teens to understand their innermost feelings, express their real selves, and achieve their goals.

6. Books we recommend for parents:

52 Simple Ways to Build Your Child's Self-Esteem and Confidence by Jan Dargatz (Nashville, TN: Oliver-Nelson, 1991). Fifty-two easy-to-do, day-by-day suggestions that a parent can put into action to help their child believe in his or her own abilities and face tomorrow with confidence.

Between Parent and Child by Haim Ginott (New York: Macmillan, 1968). Haim Ginott was a pioneer in the arena of parent education. His ideas are still as useful as they were twenty-five years ago.

Bradshaw On: The Family by John Bradshaw (Deerfield Beach, FL: Health Communications, 1988). In a book similar to the PBS television series of the same name, Bradshaw focuses on understanding the dynamics of the family. He gives a profile of a functional and a dysfunctional family, describes compulsive families, covers the most common family ills, and provides a road map for recovery.

How to Develop Self-Esteem in Your Child: 6 Vital Ingredients by Bettie B. Young (New York: Fawcett, 1991). This book details the six essential elements for developing a lasting sense of personal worth in children (of all ages) and offers a practical framework for parents in developing self-esteem in our children.

How to Give Your Child a Great Self-Image by Deborah Phillips and Fred Bernstein (New York: Plume, 1991). Teaches parents how to teach their children to feel worthy and important, how to face rejection without pain, and how to build a positive self-image.

How to Raise Teenagers' Self-Esteem by Harris Clemes and Reynold Bean (Los Angeles: Price Stern Sloan, 1978). This resource book offers practical techniques and uses case examples to illustrate new approaches to teenage problems in an easy-to-understand, straightforward style. It includes analyses of self-esteem problems, sound advice from family counselors, and guides to raising self-esteem.

How to Raise Children's Self-Esteem by Harris Clemes and Reynold Bean (Los Angeles: Price Stern Sloan, 1978). This resource book offers practical techniques for dealing with children who have learning and/or behavioral problems. This handbook will help you teach children how they can improve their self-confidence, values, and attitudes as well as increase interaction with others.

How to Talk So Kids Will Listen and Listen So Kids Will Talk by Adele Faber and Elaine Mazlish (New York: Avon, 1980). This nationally recognized resource is used as a text in many parent groups. It will teach you four skills to use to avoid turning simple conversations into arguments, five ways to instruct rather than criticize, and seven alternatives to punishment that build self-respect. Based on the work of Haim Ginott. Also available as an audio cassette, group workshop kit, and participant workbook. See *The Self-Esteem Store Catalogue* for details.

Keeping Our Children Safe: Promoting Physical, Emotional, Spiritual, and Intellectual Well-Being by Bettie B. Youngs (Louisville, KY: Westminster Knox, 1992). Of all our parenting actions, what are most important? This very thorough and nourishing book is a blueprint for instilling a real sense of wholeness in our children and in ourselves.

On Base! The Step-by-Step Self-Esteem Program For Children—Birth to 18 by Barb Friedman and Cheri Brooks. Available from The Self-Esteem Store, 3201 S.W. 15th Street, Deerfield Beach, FL 33442-8190). Developed and field tested by 36 leading authorities in child care. Short, simple, and positive activities to do and share with a child. Activities are divided into 15 levels from birth to age 18 and are constructed on the core building blocks of self-esteem. The first book to build self-esteem from birth.

Parent Effectiveness Training by Thomas Gordon (New York: Peter H. Wyden, 1970). This is one of the first and still the best book written about a respectful way of interacting with kids. Highly recommended.

Predictive Parenting: What to Say When You Talk to Your Kids by Shad Helmstetter (New York: William Morrow, 1989). This nationally recognized expert on self-talk shows how, by using positive rather than negative words, you can give your children the foundation they need to create a fulfilling life. You'll learn how to replace negative messages with powerful positive ones on such topics as drugs, alcohol, peers, self-esteem, and many others.

Raising Self-Reliant Children in a Self-Indulgent World: Seven Building Blocks for Developing Capable Young People by H. Stephen Glenn and Jane Nelsen (Rocklin, CA: Prima Publishing, 1988). This book is valuable for teachers and parents. It shows you how to teach children to be responsible and self-reliant—not through fear and intimidation, but through the maturity of feeling accountable to one's commitments.

Safeguarding Your Teenager from the Dragons of Life: A Parent's Guide to the Adolescent Years by Bettie B. Youngs (Deerfield Beach, FL: Health Communications, 1993). Written for parents and those working with adolescents, this thorough and practical book addresses the issues faced by young people today, and provides a blueprint in helping teens successfully meet the challenges and demands in staying on track toward productive and worthwhile goals.

Self-Esteem: A Family Affair by Jean Ilsley Clark (Minneapolis, MN: Winston Press, 1978). Jean Clark is a master parenting educator whose theory of nurture and structure has informed much of our own work in self-esteem. This book is a must-read for anyone serious about self-esteem development in children.

The Big—R: Responsibility, Cultivating and Encouraging Responsible Behavior by Gene Bedley. People Wise Productions, 14252 East Mall, Irvine, CA 92714. Full of ideas and activities that create responsible kids. The principles work with two-year-olds to eighteen-year-olds. Great for parents. Discover the difference that makes a difference in effective homes.

The Magic of Encouragement: Nurturing Your Child's Self-Esteem by Stephanie Marston (New York: William Morrow, 1990). Written with warmth and wit, this book provides a clear understanding of why and many practical activities for how to raise self-esteem in children of any age. This is an important book.

The Magical Child by Joseph Chilton Pearce (New York: E. P. Dutton, 1977). This is another classic book that describes the farthest reaches of human potential in children. This is some of the most interesting reading we have ever done. Highly recommended.

The New Peoplemaking (because you want to be a better parent), by Virginia Satir (Palo Alto, CA: Science and Behavior Books, 1972, revised recently). This is a profound look at how to raise high-self-esteem kids by one of the self-esteem movement's founders. Virginia was an important mentor to us.

The Winning Family: Increasing Self-Esteem in Your Children and Yourself by Louise Hart (Oakland,

CA: LifeSkills Press, 1990). This is a wonderful, easy-to-read book full of wisdom and practical things you can do to raise kids with high self-esteem. Focuses on the personal development of parents and children, how to build a strong family unit, how to protect and build an esteem-building environment, parenting responses that affect esteem, dsicipline without damage, and cultural barriers to self-esteem.

Your Child's Self-Esteem by Dorothy Corkille Briggs (Garden City, NY: Doubleday, 1970). We are still enthusiastic about this gem of a book. It is the classic parenting book on self-esteem and is still the best overview ever written. We highly recommend it to both parents and teachers.

7. Parenting programs:

We believe no school should attempt a self-esteem program without also offering self-esteem training to the students' parents. Here are some of the best programs available.

Active Parenting Today by Michael Popkin. Active Parenting Publishers, 810 Franklin Court, Suite B, Marietta, GA 30067 (Phone: 800-825-0060). Completely revised and updated for the 1990s, this new video based program for parents of two- to twelve-year-olds incorporates the latest information and techniques for successful parenting skills and substance abuse prevention. Michael is a child and family therapist and founder of Active Parenting Publishers, as well as author of *Active Parenting Discussion Program, Active Parenting of Teens* and several best-selling parent education books. Write for their complete catalogue.

International Network for Children and Families, P.O. Box 7236, Gainesville, FL 32605 (Phone: 904-377-2176; fax 904-338-3536), is a worldwide organization committed to creating new generations of responsible children that have higher self-esteem and better cooperation skills. Based on the work of psychologist Alfred Adler and Dr. Rudolf Dreikurs and on the later work of Kathryn J. Kvols and Bill Riedler, authors of *Redirecting Children's Misbehavior,* INCAF provides programs, materials, and ongoing parenting groups. We have worked directly with INCAF and totally support their work. Write or call for information about instructors in your area.

Louise Hart, Lifeskills Associates, Box 324, Boulder, CO 80306 (Phone: 303-443-6105), the author of *The Winning Family: Increasing Self-Esteem in Your Children and Yourself,* is available to present her program *Win–Win Kids in a Win–Lose World* to your district's parents. Call for her brochure.

Stephanie Marston. Raising Miracles Educational Seminars, 134 E Santa Fe Avenue, Santa Fe, New Mexico 87501 (Phone: 505-989-7596). Stephanie is the president of Raising Miracles Educational Seminars and has been a leader in the field of parent education and self-esteem for over ten years. As a consultant, therapist, and seminar leader, she is masterful at helping parents discover tools for creating more fulfilling relationships with their children. Stephanie has taught parents, teachers, and administrators nationwide. She is the author of *Parenting for High Self-Esteem* and *The Magic of Encouragement—Nurturing Your Child's Self-Esteem,* both which are available from Raising Miracles Educational Seminars.

P.E.T.: Parent Effectiveness Training. 531 Stevens Avenue, Solana Beach, CA 92705-2093 (Phone: 800-628-1197). This course, designed by Dr. Thomas Gordon, teaches parents how to raise their children in a democratic environment using the communication skills of Active

Listening, I-Messages, and the No Lose Conflict Resolution Method to solve family conflicts. Research has proved that children are more confident, are more emotionally stable, have healthier self-esteem, and will be better prepared to be mature adults who take responsibility for their own lives when raised with P.E.T. Parents can learn P.E.T. by taking a class from an authorized instructor or by purchasing the P.E.T. Home Program. Call for more information.

The STEP Programs by Don Dinkmeyer, Gary D. McKay, and James S. Dinkmeyer. Available from American Guidance Service, P.O. Box 99, Circle Pines, MN 55014-1796 (Phone: 800-328-2560). The STEP programs, STEP, STEP/Teen, Early Childhood STEP, Next STEP, and now Early Childhood STEP Spanish Language Edition—are an easy, effective way for you to help parents improve relationships in their families. The main foci are encouragement and communication. Again, write for their complete brochure.

8. Women, girls, and self-esteem:

The Confidence Factor: How Self-Esteem Can Change Your Life by Judith Briles (New York: Master Media Limited, 1990). Explores why women so often feel an utter lack of self-confidence and have an unjustifiably poor opinion of themselves. Learn about the Ten Commandments of self-confidence, working through personal crisis, women at work, and the balancing act—keeping it all together.

The Woman's Comfort Book, A Self-Nurturing Guide for Restoring Balance by Jennifer Louden (San Francisco: Harper San Francisco, 1992). Nurturance comes naturally to most women—as long as it is directed at someone else. Taking care of yourself is more difficult—here are 200 soothing recipes for relaxation, self-care, gentle growth, and personal satisfaction.

Women and Self-Esteem, Understanding and Improving the Way We Think and Feel about Ourselves by Linda Sanford and Mary Donovan. Available from The Self-Esteem Store, 3201 S.W. 15th Street, Deerfield Beach, FL 33442-8190. For every woman who has ever wanted to like herself more. This book examines how women's harmful attitudes about themselves are shaped and offers ways to resolve this dilemma by building higher self-esteem. A truly valuable and effective guide to women's esteem issues.

Women and Self-Esteem: A Video Program by Linda Sanford. Available from Nicolas J. Kaufman Productions, 14 Clyde St., Newtonville, MA 02160 (Phone: 617-964-4466). This 28-minute video is a documentary of a workshop led by a coauthor of the book, Linda Sanford. A group of 75 women participate in psychological exercises and discussion designed to enhance self-esteem. Issues of racism, ageism, sexism, and stereotypes of women with disabilities are addressed.

9. Multicultural self-esteem curriculum materials:

Developing Positive Self-Images and Discipline in Black Children by Jawanza Kunjufu. Chicago, IL: African-American Images, 1984 (Phone: 800-552-1991). Jawanza Kunjufu is an educational consultant with African-American Images. He is constantly on the lecture circuit, with over thirty different workshops, addressing students, parents, teachers, and community residents; in preschools, elementary schools, high schools, colleges, and churches.

The Journal of Emotional and Behavioral Problems, National Educational Service, 1610 West Third St., P.O. Box 8, Bloomington, IN 47402-0008 (Phone: 812-336-7700). This magazine is dedicated to networking and supporting those involved with reclaiming children and youth in family, school, and community: They define reclaiming as recognizing the worth of what has been devalued, restoring, and empowering in environments of belonging, mastery, independence, and generosity. $35.00/year.

Growing Up Black and Proud (Grades 9–12) by Peter Bell. Available from the Attainment Company, P.O. Box 930160, Verona, WI 53593-0160 (Phone: 800-327-4269). This curriculum is designed to help African-American teens discover who they are and succeed to the best of their ability without using drugs or alcohol. Includes a user-friendly guide for teens. The teen guide text is richly illustrated and filled with stories, real-life examples, and engaging activities. The curriculum is easy to follow and leads instructors through fourteen sessions that correspond to the teen guide.

Impact!: A Self-Esteem-Based Skill Development Program for Secondary Students by Gerry Dunne, Dianne Schilling, and David Cowan. Available from Innerchoice Publishing, P.O. Box 2476, Spring Valley, CA 92077 (Phone: 619-698-2437). *IMPACT!* increases the ability of students to function effectively in a multicultural environment and encourages them to recognize their broader roles as members of society. The curriculum guide includes units on communicating effectively, self-awareness, making decisions, resolving conflicts, taking responsibility, managing stress, setting and attaining goals, solving problems, relating to peers, team building, and careers. It features the "circle session," discussion process, and many experiential activities, along with theory information and step-by-step procedures for circle leadership—including student leadership. Individualized worksheets, also available in Spanish, are provided in each unit.

Mission Star: A Self-Esteem Based Gang Prevention Bilingual Curriculum (Grades 3–4, can be modified for K–12) by Lulu Lopez, Ph.D. Available from The Self-Esteem Store, 3201 S.W. 15th Street, Deerfield Beach, FL 33442-8190. This bilingual curriculum counters low self-esteem and lack of responsibility, two major causes of gang affiliation. Activities and strategies for building self-esteem and understanding the nature and consequences of gang involvement.

Positively Different: Creating a Bias-Free Environment for Young Children by Ana Consuelo Matiella, MA. Available from ETR Associates, P.O. Box 1830, Santa Cruz, CA 95061-1830 (Phone: 800-321-4407). *Positively Different* gives elementary school teachers, parents, and other caregivers practical suggestions to teach young children to recognize, respect, and celebrate diversity and to help children take pride in their "cultural selves." Help children recognize that "different" means unique, special, and important!

SETCLAE: Self-Esteem through Culture Leads to Academic Excellence by African American Images, 9204 Commercial Avenue, Suite 308, Chicago, IL 60617 (Phone: 800-552-1991). SETCLAE is an extremely comprehensive, Afrocentric, multicultural curriculum available for schools K–12. SETCLAE provides lesson plans, workbooks, text and supplementary books, tests, posters, awards, and videos. Preview material is available.

The Value of Respecting Others—Grades 4–8—by Amy Keller and Gene Floersch. Available from the Bureau for At-Risk Youth, Promoting Growth through Knowledge, 645 New York Avenue, Huntington, NY 11743 (Phone: 800-99-YOUTH). This book teaches children to accept themselves and others as having dignity and worth. The activities are designed to help students develop the tolerance and understanding needed to excel in today's culturally diverse society. An excellent addition to any multicultural curriculum.

279

10. Some of the best self-help books for self-esteem:

Feel the Fear and Do It Anyway by Susan Jeffers (San Diego: Harcourt Brace Jovanovich, 1987). Dynamic and inspirational! Filled with concrete techniques to turn passivity into assertiveness. You will learn: how to risk a little every day, a power vocabulary, decision-making skills, and essential visualization techniques. Turn that fear around and make it a positive!

The Psychology of Self-Esteem by Nathaniel Branden (New York: Bantam, 1971). This life-changing program is designed to facilitate self-awareness, self-acceptance, self-responsibility, and self-assertion. Covers the basics of self-esteem, living consciously, liberation from guilt, living responsibly, and nurturing the self-esteem of others. Branden's best seller—over 100,000 copies sold.

Glad to Be Me: Building Self-Esteem in Yourself and Others by Dov Peretz Elkins. Available from Growth Associates, 212 Stuart Road East, Princeton, NJ 08540 (Phone: 609-497-7375). A wonderful anthology of brief selections from Maslow, Mark Twain, Shakespeare, Tolstoy, Goethe, Emerson, Tillich, Rogers, Thoreau, Einstein, and Satir on self-acceptance, self-trust, self-affirmation, self-love, avoiding putdowns, raising self-esteem, and loving your body. A must for anyone who works with self-esteem development.

Honoring the Self: Personal Integrity and the Heroic Potentials of Human Nature by Nathaniel Branden (Los Angeles, CA: Jeremy P. Tarcher, 1983).

How to Raise Your Self-Esteem by Nathaniel Branden (New York: Bantam, 1987). A factual, action-oriented, step-by-step guide to strengthening the feeling of self-worth. Branden has distilled a lifetime of experience to create a self-help book that will change the way you live your life.

Self-Esteem by Matthew McKay, Ph.D., and P. Fanning (Oakland; CA: New Harbinger Publications, 1987). A proven program of cognitive techniques for assessing, improving, and maintaining self-esteem. One of the best on the market for adults. Shows you how to handle self-criticism, mistakes, guilt, and distorted thinking. Learn compassion, love, and acceptance for yourself. Has been used for college courses.

Getting Unstuck, Breaking through Your Barriers to Change by Sid and Suzanne Simon. Available from Values Press, P.O. Box 450, Sunderland, MA 01375 (Phone: 413-665-4800). Break through your internal barriers to change! Learn to overcome low self-esteem, indecisiveness, resistance from others, fear, and lack of willpower—and all with guidance and support. It's hard to feel good about yourself when you feel stuck in a rut.

Forgiveness, How to Make Peace with Your Past and Get on with Your Life by Sid and Suzanne Simon. Available from Values Press, P.O. Box 450, Sunderland, MA 01375 (Phone: 413-665-4800). To understand the ability to forgive is a profound emotional strength. To forgive, we do not need to forget. A guide to spiritual healing that enables us to put injustices aside and make a journey to wholeness. Shows the connection between self-esteem and the ability to forgive oneself and others.

Homecoming, Reclaiming, and Championing Your Inner Child by John Bradshaw (New York: Bantam, 1990). "Three things are striking about inner child work. The speed with which people change when they do this work; the depth of that change; the power and creativity that result." Contains a wealth of techniques and information to heal your inner child.

Negative Criticism, What You Can Do about It! by Sidney Simon, Ph.D. Available from Values Press, P.O. Box 450, Sunderland, MA 01375 (Phone: 413-665-4800). The sharp knives of criticism threaten all of us at one time or another, but with the strategies in this book, criticism can be handled in a positive way. One of Sid's real classics.

Personal Caring—A Recovery Catalogue. Available from Health Communications, Inc., 3201 S.W. 15th Street, Deerfield Beach, FL 33442–8190 (Phone: 800-851-9100). This catalogue is a wonderful guide for recovering adults. The pages of this catalogue represent the offerings of dedicated professionals who have shared their experiences and expertise in helping Health Communications bring health and happiness into our lives.

The Power of Self-Esteem by Nathaniel Branden. Available from Health Communications, Inc., 3201 S.W. 15th Street, Deerfield Beach, FL 33442-8190. In this book, Nathaniel Branden, "The Father of the Self-Esteem Movement," stresses that it is still possible to develop positive self-esteem. He explains what self-esteem *is,* where it comes from, and how we get it. This book may be the clearest, most useful, broad-based definition of self-esteem ever presented.

Healing the Child Within by Charles Whitfield, M.D. Available from Health Communications, Inc., 3201 S.W. 15th Street, Deerfield Beach, FL 33442-8190. Discovery and Recovery for Adult Children of Dysfunctional Families. With this book you can experience the gift of creating your own personal freedom in your recovery and your life.

Learning to Love Yourself: Finding Your Self-Worth by Sharon Wegscheider-Cruse. Available from Health Communications, Inc., 3201 S.W. 15th Street, Deerfield Beach, FL 33442-8190. Learning to love yourself is a powerful journey to self-worth.

Building Self-Esteem and Study Guide by L. S. Barksdale. Available from The Self-Esteem Store, 3201 S.W. 15th Street, Deerfield Beach, FL 33442-8190. This do-it-yourself book involves a rapid, direct Action Program wth the essential 3rd approach for building self-esteem. Thirteen-week study guide was prepared to assist study groups and support groups in organizing an effective program for building self-esteem.

11. Audio tapes:

Nightingale-Conant Corporation, 3700 North Lehigh Avenue, Chicago, IL 60648, publishes a series of excellent motivational and self-enhancing tapes including *How to Build High Self-Esteem* by Jack Canfield. Send for a catalogue. Our favorites are by Brian Tracy, Denis Waitley, Charles Garfield, Wayne Dyer, Bob Moawad, Tony Robbins, Leo Buscaglia, Nathaniel Branden, and a program called *The New Time Management.* They publish several new albums per month. Once you get on their mailing list, they will send you a new catalogue each month. You may also call them toll free at 1-800-323-3938.

CarrerTrack, 1800 38th Street, Boulder, CO 80301, also publishes an extensive catalogue of motivational and self-improvement audiotape albums and video programs, including *Self-Esteem and Peak Performance* by Jack Canfield. Write for their catalogue or call 303-440-7440 for more information.

A few audiocassette albums that we think are basic and important are:

How to Build High Self-Esteem by Jack Canfield. Available for $60 from Self-Esteem Seminars, 6035 Bristol Parkway, Culver City, CA 90230. This six-cassette album clarifies the holistic model of self-esteem, details the "ten steps to success" that Jack has made famous in his public seminars, and provides many practical techniques that you can use with yourself and with your students. It also contains the "Tri-Synch Integration Tape," which uses many of the latest techniques from NLP (NeuroLinguistic Programming) to deeply install the principles and practices of building high self-esteem into the subconscious mind.

Self-Esteem and Peak Performance by Jack Canfield. Available for $60 from Self-Esteem Seminars, 6035 Bristol Parkway, Culver City, CA 90230. This six-cassette album is a highly motivational as well as educational experience. It contains a live seminar recorded in Boulder, Colorado. In addition to four and a half hours of information on how to build high self-esteem and increase your levels of peak performance, it also contains a powerful affirmations tape and over an hour of live questions and answers.

Self-Esteem in the Classroom by Jack Canfield. Available from Self-Esteem Seminars, 6035 Bristol Parkway, Culver City, CA 90230. This three-cassette album contains four and a half hours of a live seminar on how to build high self-esteem in the classroom. It is appropriate for teachers, counselors, and administrators. Listening to this album would add a great deal of depth to what has been presented in this book.

Building Self-Esteem in the Classroom: The Experts Speak features six one-hour presentations by Jack Canfield, Sidney B. Simon, Hanoch McCarty, Connie Dembrowsky, Frank Siccone, and the team of Peggy Bielen and Sandy McDaniel. Available for $50 from Self-Esteem Seminars, 6035 Bristol Parkway, Culver City, CA 90230. This album provides six different perspectives on teaching self-esteem from the nation's leading experts. All have been members of the Board of Trustees of the National Council for Self-Esteem, and all are leading educational consultants and self-esteem curriculum developers.

Unlocking Your Potential (Ages 13–18) by Bob Moawad. Available from Nightingale-Conant, 3700 North Lehigh Avenue, Chicago, IL 60648. This audio program for teens gives youth the direction they seek, and just when they need it most. Coming from a professional educator and based on the latest studies of peak achievers and their winning attitudes, it helps teens learn to take charge of their lives, set goals, and develop action plans. Fun to listen to! Write for the complete Nightingale-Conant catalogue.

Developing Capable People by H. Stephen Glenn. Available from Sunrise Books and Tapes, Box B, Provo, UT 84603. This six-cassette album introduces you to the significant seven skills and perceptions that are necessary for developing capable people. These seven skills include developing self-discipline, judgment, responsibility, intrapersonal and interpersonal communication, a sense of personal significance, and systemic skills.

12. Videotapes:

Building Self-Esteem by Robert Reasoner. Sunburst Publications, 39 Washington Avenue, P.O. Box 40, Pleasantville, NY 10570-0040 (Phone: 800-431-1934, ext. 1221). This video shows how a self-esteem emphasis can be integrated into middle school and high school.

I Like Being Me: Self-Esteem by Sunburst Communications, 39 Washington Ave., P.O. Box 40, Pleasantville, NY 10570-0040 (Phone: 800-431-1934). Using compelling scenarios, this program shows how self-esteem is fostered by positive feelings or held back by negative feelings, and how it can be changed.

Self-Esteem and Peak Performance by Jack Canfield. Available for $139 from Self-Esteem Seminars, 6035 Bristol Parkway, Culver City, CA 90230 (Phone: 800-2-ESTEEM). This two volume, three-hour VHS video training program is an excellent resource for a staff inservice or simply to lend out to individual teachers and counselors. It covers the basic concepts and techniques required to raise self-esteem in yourself and others. It also provides a detailed description of the "ten steps to success."

Self-Esteem: Elementary Grades by Robert Reasoner. Sunburst Publications, 39 Washington Avenue, P.O. Box 40, Pleasantville, NY 10570-0040 (Phone: 800-431-1934, ext. 1221). This is a staff development video with a study guide developed by Michele Borba. It illustrates how different schools have approached the implementation of self-esteem. The guide enables a school staff to use the video as a basis for discussion.

Self-Esteem in the Classroom by Jack Canfield. Available for $59 from Self-Esteem Seminars, 6035 Bristol Parkway, Culver City, CA 90230. This two-hour VHS video is also excellent for a teacher inservice or for individual viewing. It covers the basic theory of building self-esteem in educational settings and provides instructions for the most important esteem-building activities.

Staff Development: Building Self-Esteem by Sunburst Communications, 39 Washington Avenue, P.O. Box 40, Pleasantville, NY 10570-0040 (Phone: 800-431-1934). Viewers hear from teachers, administrators, and students in two schools with successful self-esteem programs, and explore the ideas and concepts that make these programs work.

The Power of Choice by Michael Pritchard. Available from The Self-Esteem Store, 3201 S.W. 15th Street, Deerfield Beach, FL 33442-8190. *The Power of Choice* is a twelve-part video series focusing on self-esteem, responsibility, depression and suicide, parents, and other important topics to teens. Comedian/teen counselor Pritchard discusses a wide variety of contemporary issues with teens. Each video has an instructors guide with written assignments, discussion points, and learning activities. The tapes can be purchased individually or as a series. Write or call 1-800-831-6064 for a catalogue.

The STAR Program by Jack Canfield. Available from Self-Esteem Seminars, 6035 Bristol Parkway, Culver City, CA 90230 (Phone: 800-2-ESTEEM). This is a video-based intensive three-day personal and professional development program. It utilizes five hours of video and a 120-page participant manual. It is taught by in-house trainers who are trained by Jack Canfield and his staff. Each participant receives a six-cassette album as a follow-up and reinforcement program. This is a very powerful program. Write or call for a more complete brochure.

Stress and Energy in the Learning Process by Hanoch McCarty. Available from Self-Esteem Seminars, Inc., 6035 Bristol Parkway, Culver City, CA 90230 (Phone: 800-2-ESTEEM). Let Dr. McCarty help you to discover what motivates kids to learn. You will learn how to reduce classroom stress and calm tense and hyper kids. You will also learn the single greatest motivation for learning. This is a new approach to classroom management.

Unlocking Your Potential by Bob Moawad. Available from Edge Learning Institute, 2212 N. 30th, #200, Tacoma, WA 98403 (Phone: 206-272-3103). This is a video-based self-development program to develop decision-making skills, goal-setting skills, self-esteem, and motivation in junior high and high school students. This is an excellent program. Make sure to write for a catalogue.

You Can Choose! by Michael Pritchard. Available from The Self-Esteem Store, 3201 S.W. 15th Street, Deerfield Beach, FL 33442-8190. This ten-part video series builds self-esteem and improves social skills for children six to ten years old. Music, skits, and comic characters make the videos fun, while each episode addresses an important social issue. Write for a complete catalogue.

Developing Capable People by H. Stephen Glenn. Available from The Self-Esteem Store, 3201 S.W. 15th Street, Deerfield Beach, FL 33442-8190. One of the most outstanding programs in the country. Teaches the Significant Seven perceptions and skills that young people must acquire in order to live productive and successful lives. Excellent for parents and teachers—will change the way you perceive people and children.

Developing Healthy Self-Esteem by H. Stephen Glenn. Available from The Self-Esteem Store, 3201 S.W. 15th Street, Deerfield Beach, FL 33442-8190. Points out weaknesses in many popular approaches to self-esteem and suggests an alternative model that emphasizes self-respect and self-actualization.

13. A unique and valuable elementary school resource:

Beth Pergola, 7049 Brown Derby Circle, Las Vegas, NV 89128 (Phone: 702-363-6749). Beth is a classroom teacher who has written hundreds of songs for teaching self-esteem and accelerating the learning of basic elementary subject matter. We have seen Beth's kids perform these songs, and we were deeply moved. What's more important is that days later we were still singing those same songs. We had picked up the lyrics that fast—and so do the kids. Beth currently has three tapes available. They each come with a booklet that contains the words to each of the songs. The cost is $11.00 per tape.

Sing It Instead. (1980). Classroom-tested songs that are useful in teaching math, science, social studies, and whole language skills.

Sing It Instead 2. (1985). More classroom-tested songs to teach subject matter.

Self-Esteem. (1990). Four children's songs that lift self-esteem. The songs are *Wonderful Me; Yeah, Yeah, It's Another Day; I'm A Grump; and I've Got Self-Esteem.*

14. Organizations you should know about:

We suggest that you buy a stack of postcards or photocopy a form letter and send one to all of the following organizations asking them to send you a brochure and place you on their mailing list. The materials you receive will keep you up to date on what is going on in the field and how the various organizations can meet your personal and professional needs.

The National Council for Self-Esteem, P.O. Box 277877, Sacramento, CA 95827-7877. NCSE is a nonprofit membership organization dedicated to bringing you the latest information on self-esteem resources, research, and upcoming conferences through their quarterly newsletter, *Self-Esteem Today*. At the time of this writing, there are thirty-five state and local chapters, which hold regular meetings and local conferences. The organization has held state and national conferences in Alaska, Arizona, Arkansas, California, Florida, Hawaii, Maryland, Michigan, Missouri, Nevada, New York, Ohio, Oregon, and Virginia. Its international division has also cosponsored conferences in Norway, Great Britain, and Russia. Membership in only $30 per year—a bargain for all the services that you receive.

The International Alliance for Invitational Education, School of Education, Curry Building, University of North Carolina at Greensboro, Greensboro, NC 27412. Based on the work of Dr. William Purkey, who wrote *Inviting School Success* and *Self-Esteem and School Achievement*, the Alliance publishes a journal, a newsletter, disseminates announcements of new books and resources, sponsors workshops and an annual conference, provides inservice training, and makes awards each year to outstanding schools and educators. Dues are $25 per year.

The Center for the Study of Self-Esteem, P.O. Box 1532, Santa Cruz, CA 95061. Sponsors the Annual Northern California Self-Esteem Conference (usually during the last weekend of February), publishes a quarterly newsletter, provides consultants, and disseminates information on curriculum resources.

The Foundation for Self-Esteem, 6035 Bristol Parkway, Culver City, CA 90230 (Phone: 310-568-1505). The Foundation distributes educational materials; develops video programs; conducts inservice trainings for schools, school districts, and professional associations; and awards the "Golden Apple Awards" each year to individuals who have made an outstanding contribution to furthering self-esteem in education. Distributes *The Goals Program*, a video-based self-esteem and self-sufficiency program for adults at risk. The program is currently in use in numerous community colleges, in thirty-eight county welfare programs in the United States and Canada, and in the Maryland State Prison.

Global Alliance for Transforming Education, 4202 Ashwoody Trail, Atlanta, GA 30319 (Phone: 404-458-5678; fax 404-454-9749). Phil Gang, Ph.D., executive director. This is a consortium of educators working together to transform education along self-esteem and holistic lines. Write for a brochure.

The National Self-Esteem Resources and Development Center, 176 Corte Anita, Greenbrae, CA 94904 (Phone: 415-461-3401). This is the headquarters of *The Esteem Team* (Judith Feldman, founder and executive director). They have training, curriculum materials, a newsletter, and a music tape available. Their music cassette *B.E.S.T. Friends: Songs for Children about Friendship, Cooperation and Self-Esteem* is truly a delight.

Self-Esteem Seminars, 6035 Bristol Parkway, Culver City, CA 90230 (Phone: 800-2-ESTEEM). Jack Canfield, the president of Self-Esteem Seminars, conducts school inservice trainings, distributes curricula, tapes, and books on self-esteem development; offers weekend workshops to the general public for the development of self-esteem in Los Angeles, San Diego, and St. Louis; and conducts a seven-day Self-Esteem Facilitating Skills Training Program every summer to train people to conduct self-esteem seminars.

Sunrise Books, Tapes and Videos, P.O. Box B, Provo, UT 84603 (Phone: 800-456-7770, 801-377-2800). This is the organization that sponsors the workshops and distributes the materials of H. Stephen Glenn, Jane Nelsen, and Lynn Lott, three of the most influential teachers in the self-esteem movement today. Their seminars, books, tapes, and videos are excellent resources for self-development and staff development. They also publish a wonderful quarterly newsletter ($6 per year, free with purchase of materials). Their two best books to start out with are *Positive Discipline* and *Raising Self-Reliant Children in a Self-Indulgent World.*

The California Council to Promote Self-Esteem and Responsibility, 313 Del Oro Avenue, Davis, CA 95616 (Phone: 916-756-8678). This is a California-based organization designed to implement the findings of the former California Self-Esteem Task Force. It publishes a newsletter and a journal and holds periodic meetings, conferences, and trainings in the area of promoting self-esteem.

Institute for Reality Therapy, 7301 Medical Center Drive, Suite 104, Canoga Park, CA 91307 (Phone: 818-888-0688). William Glasser offers trainings in reality therapy and schools without failure. Write for more information on his fine programs.

The Society for Accelerative Learning and Teaching (SALT)/21st Century Learning Systems, 3028 Emerson Avenue South, Minneapolis, MN 55408 (Phone: 612-827-4856). Offers a journal, a newsletter, and an annual conference for people dedicated to improving educational performance through accelerative learning, which is based on the work of Dr. Georgi Lozanov and featured in the book *Superlearning* by Ostrander and Schroeder. As accelerative learning occurs, self-esteem improves greatly. This is a very dynamic and exciting organization.

15. Self-Esteem Consultants:

The authors are both available as consultants, trainers, and speakers and would love to receive your inquiries. We can be reached at the following addresses and phone numbers;

Jack Canfield, Self-Esteem Seminars, 6035 Bristol Parkway, Culver City, CA 90230 (Phone: 800-2-ESTEEM; 310-337-9222; fax: 310-337-7465) Jack conducts training workshops for administrators, teachers, counselors, and parents. He also delivers powerful and inspirational conference and back-to-school keynotes. He has conducted over two hundred conference keynotes and has conducted inservice trainings for over five hundred schools and school districts throughout the United States, Canada, Europe, and Australia. His topics include "Self-Esteem in the Classroom," "Self-Esteem and the At-Risk Student," "Self-Esteem and Peak Performance," "Counseling Skills for Building Self-Esteem," "Parenting for High Self-Esteem," "How to Build High Self-Esteem in Yourself and Others," and "Chicken Soup for the Soul."

Wells Associates, 2228 Kaukauna Court, Traverse City, MI 49684 (Phone: 616-929-2464; fax: 616-941-2250). Dr. Harold Clive Wells, Ann Colleen Wells, and Dr. Lillian Stover Wells are widely experienced university professors, writers, and consultants. They specialize in teaching, lecturing, and advising on parenting skills, small business management, self-esteem, interpersonal communication, and research. Wells Associates are particularly known for their ability to convey their teachings with humor and inclusiveness.

We would also like to give you information on how to contact twelve other outstanding presenters and trainers in self-esteem. We recommend these people to you without any hesitation whatsoever. Write each of them requesting their speaking brochures and current fee schedules. Several of them offer intensive summer trainings you can attend as well.

Peggy Bielen, Enhancing Educations, Inc., P.O. Box 16001, Newport Beach, CA 92659 (Phone: 800-756-7856, 714-756-2226). Peggy is an internationally recognized speaker on self-esteem, parenting, discipline, and teaching strategies. Her presentations integrate information and audience involvement in an engaging format that teaches practical skills. She has delighted thousands of administrators, teachers, counselors and parents with topics such as *Creating a Positive Learning Environment, Skills for Building Healthy Self-Esteem, Self-Esteem: Let's Get Practical, Self-Esteem: Meeting the Challenge of At-Risk Students,* and *Helping Our Children Feel Lovable and Capable.* She coauthored *Project Self-Esteem,* a parent-involvement curriculum for improving self-esteem and preventing substance abuse.

Jane Bluestein, Ph.D., Instructional Support Services, Inc., 160 Washington, SE, Suite 64, Albuquerque, NM 87108 (Phone: 800-688-1960, 505-255-3007). She is an expert on creating healthy, functional adult–child relationships that encourage responsibility, self-esteem, self-management, achievement, problem solving, and conflict resolution. Author of *21st Century Discipline, Being a Successful Teacher,* and *Parents, Teens and Boundaries,* Jane offers practical, humorous, and down-to-earth programs for educators, counselors, and parents.

Michele Borba, 840 Prescott Drive, Palm Springs, CA 92262 (Phone: 619-323-5387). Michele is the author of *Esteem Builders: A K–8 Self-Esteem Curriculum.* Michele is an excellent presenter and consultant who has facilitated several long-term school transformation programs. Her depth of knowledge on self-esteem in education is unmatched by anyone else we know.

Connie Dembrowski, Institute for Affective Skill Development, P.O. Box 880, La Luz, NM 88337 (Phone: 402-423-1623). Connie knows more about developing self-esteem and responsibility with at-risk youth than anyone we know. She is the author of *Self-Esteem* and *Personal and Social Responsibility,* two highly effective programs for developing self-esteem and internal motivation in adolescents. Write for a brochure on her materials and her consulting.

Gail Dusa, 6641 Leyland Park Drive, San Jose, CA 95120 (Phone: 800-GET-DUSA). Gail is a nationally recognized keynote speaker, workshop leader, author, and educational consultant. She specializes in practical strategies for building self-esteem cooperative learning, increasing personal confidence, goal setting, and group facilitation for schools in the process of restructuring. Gail is a motivational speaker who, with humor and charm, emphasizes practical strategies for implementing cooperative learning and for building self-esteem. Her publications include *Building Self-Esteem in Secondary Schools.*

Bob Harris, Esteem for Excellence, 5942 Edinger Avenue, Suite 113, Huntington Beach, CA 92649 (Phone: 714-373-9911; fax: 714-373-9011). Bob is a noted authority on self-esteem, multicultural education, and the prevention of and intervention in gangs and drugs. Bob is also a trainer of "Dimensions of Learning," a framework that teaches how to integrate an esteeming environment, learning-centered instruction, and critical and creative thinking with curriculum. His publications include *Self-Esteem—The Same in Any Language: A Multicultural Curriculum,* and the innovative *My Goal and Victory Journal.*

Hanoch McCarty, P.O. Box 66, Galt, CA 95632 (Phone: 800-231-7353). Hanoch is one of the most creative and effective presenters and workshop leaders in America. His keynote addresses literally mesmerize an audience: people are transfixed and delighted. His work is filled with startling insights, thought-provoking concepts, and especially, practical and useful strategies and approaches. His programs are unique in their level of appropriate humor and in their effective results. He presents to teachers, administrators, parents, and teen groups with equal facility.

William Purkey, Professor of Education, University of North Carolina at Greensboro, Professor of Counselor Education, Curry Building, UNCG, Greensboro, NC 27412 (Phone: 919-334-5100). Dr. Purkey is one of the most profound thinkers and presenters in the area of self-esteem that we know of. His presentations always inspire us, motivate us, and give us practical ways to operationalize everything we believe about self-esteem.

Robert Reasoner, Self-Esteem Resources, 234 Montgomery Lane, Port Ludlow, WA 98365 (Phone: 206-437-0300). Robert Reasoner is a former school superintendent who transformed his district by focusing on the self-esteem development of its staff and students. He served as director of the California Center for Self-Esteem and later helped to found the National Council for Self-Esteem. He is the author of *Building Self-Esteem: A Comprehensive Program for Schools* and *Building Self-Esteem in Secondary Schools* as well as the *Student Self-Esteem Inventory.* Bob is known for his effective keynotes and workshops for administrators, teachers, and parents.

Rich Revheim, 1384 Finch Avenue, Tulare, CA 93274 (Phone: 209-686-5732). Rich is a dynamic presenter and coauthor of *Personality Fitness Training.* Rich has a wide variety of in-service programs on self-esteem development that he can provide for your school, district, or conference.

Frank Siccone, The Siccone Institute, 2151 Union Street, San Francisco, CA 94123 (Phone: 415-922-2244). Frank is the coauthor with Jack Canfield of the two-volume activity guide *101 Ways to Develop Student Self-Esteem and Responsibility.* Frank is a genius in the area of teaching educators and others how to take greater responsibility for their lives and achieve more of their goals. Inservice workshops are available for administrators, teachers, students, and parents in educational leadership, self-esteem and responsibility, communication and teamwork, and the teacher as coach.

Sidney B. Simon, 45 Old Mountain Road, Hadley, MA 01035 (Phone: 413-584-4382). Sid was Jack's professor at the University of Massachusetts when Jack was first learning about enhancing self-esteem in the classroom. Sid is the coauthor of *The IALAC Story, Negative Criticism,* and *Getting Unstuck,* among many other best-selling books. Sid's compassion, years of experience, and commitment to practical classroom applications make his workshops some of the most sought after in the nation. Sid also conducts several summer intensive trainings.

16. Tests and inventories for evaluating self-esteem[1]:

The evaluation of self-esteem is not an easy task. Yet it is essential in determining the status of student self-esteem or the effectiveness of any efforts at intervention. There are several ways to approach this challenge. First, the impact of self-esteem programs can be inferred through gathering data and comparing such data over periods of time. Although it is difficult to attribute changes solely to self-esteem, such statistics can be very significant.

---

[1] We wish to thank Robert Reasoner, former president of the National Council for Self-Esteem, for helping us with this section of the bibliography. He did most of the research and the annotations.

Second, self-esteem can be determined by asking students direct questions about how they feel, using self-report measures. However, such instruments are not recommended for students below fourth grade, and even the validity of scores of fourth-graders might be questioned.

Third, levels of self-esteem can be inferred by observing the behaviors of students and by interpreting what students say about themselves. It is recommended that different sources of data be used to determine the validity of the information gathered. The following instruments and processes are offered as suggestions:

A. Informal measures that might reflect self-esteem:

Achievement as measured by standardized tests
Attendance: Unexcused absences or average daily rate
Awards, honors, or distinctions earned
Crimes reported
Discipline referral rate
Dropout rate
Incidence of drug or alcohol use
Parent or staff surveys
Percentage of students entering college from high school
Referrals to rehabilitation clinics
Number of suspensions or expulsions
Teacher observations
Vandalism rates: Amount spent per year per school

B. The most widely used self-esteem self-report assessment instruments:

Children's Self-Concept Scale by Piers & Harris (Grades 3–12), Counselor Recordings and Tests, Box 6148, Acklen Station, Nashville, TN 37212. Provides scores for General Self, Behavior, Intellect, Physical, Anxiety, Popularity, and Happiness and Satisfaction.

Culture Free Self-Esteem Inventories by James Battle (Grades 3–9), Special Child Publications, 4535 Union Bay, Seattle, WA 98105. Provides information on characteristics measured: Social/ Peer, Academic/School, Parents/Home.

Self-Concept and Motivational Inventory (SCAMIN) by Farrah, Milchus, & Reitz (Age 4–K, Grades Primary 1–3, Intermediate Grades 3–6, Secondary Grades 7–12), PERSON-O-METRICS, 20504 Williamsburg Road, Dearborn Heights, MI 48127. Characteristics measured: Achievement Investment, Failure Avoidance, Total Motivation, Role Expectation, Self-Adequacy, Total Self-Concept.

Self-Esteem Inventories (SEI) by Stanley Coopersmith (Grades 3–12), Consulting Psychologists Press, 3803 East Bayshore Road, Palo Alto, CA 94303. Provides Total Self Score as well as subscores for General Self, Social Self, Home–Parents, School–Academic, and a Lie scale. Forms: School Form—grades 3–12; Short Form—Ages 8–15; Adult Form.

Self Observational Scales by Stenner & Katzenmeyer (Grades K–3, Intermediate 4–6, Junior High 7–9, Senior High 10–12), NTS Research Corporation, 2634 Chapel Hill Boulevard, Durham,

NC 27707. Provides scores for Self: Acceptance and Security; Social: Maturity and Confidence; Affiliation: School, Teacher, and Peer with forms for Primary K–3, Intermediate 4–6, Junior High 7–9, and Senior High 10–12.

Student Self-Esteem Inventory (SSEI) by Robert Reasoner and Ragnar Gilberts (Grades 4–12), Educational Data Systems, 90 Great Oaks Boulevard, San Jose, CA 95119. Provides Total Score and subscores for Security, Identity, Belonging, Purpose, and Personal Competence. All items refer to classroom, so it is especially effective in evaluating school program effectiveness.

Tennessee Self-Concept Scale by William Fitts (12 years old to adult), Counselor Recordings and Tests, Box 6148, Acklen Station, Nashville, TN 37212. Especially appropriate for use in a clinical setting. Provides nine subscores for self-esteem, including family, moral, behavior, social, etc.

C. Observational measures of self-esteem:

A Process for Assessment of Effective Student Functioning by Lambert, Hartsough, & Bower (Grades K–7), Publishers Test Service, CTB/McGraw-Hill, 2500 Garden Road, Monterey, CA 93940. Characteristics measured: Pupil Behavior Rating Scale–Teacher Ratings (K–3) Peer and Self Ratings (3–7).

Behavioral Academic Self-Esteem (BASE) by S. Coopersmith and Ragnar Gilberts (Grades K–8), Consulting Psychologists Press, 3803 E. Bayshore, Palo Alto, CA 94303. This is an observation scale to be used by the teacher who is asked to rate the child's behavior on sixteen items. Subscores are provided for Student Initiative, Social Attention, Success/Failure, Social Attraction, Self-Confidence, and Total Academic Self. Can be especially valuable when used in conjunction with a self-report form.

Florida Key by Purkey, Cage, and Graves (Grades K–6), University of North Carolina, School of Education, Greensboro, NC 27412. Characteristics measured: Relating, Asserting, Investing, Coping, Total Learner Self.